American Silver

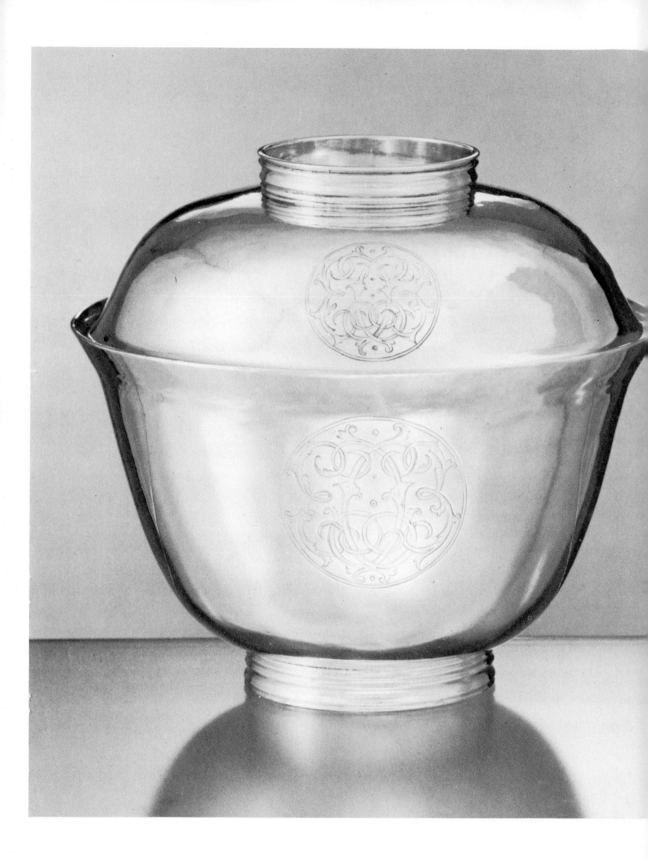

American Silver

A HISTORY OF STYLE, 1650–1900

Graham Hood

E. P. DUTTON  NEW YORK

Facing the title page: Sugar bowl, ca. 1738–45, by Simeon Soumain; H. 4 3/16 inches. Yale University Art Gallery, New Haven, Connecticut. The Mabel Brady Garvan Collection.

On page 8: Vase, 1894, by Tiffany and Company; H. 17 7/8 inches. Museum of the City of New York. Gift of Harry Harkness Flagler.

For
Gale
Sarah and Jorin
with love

Contents

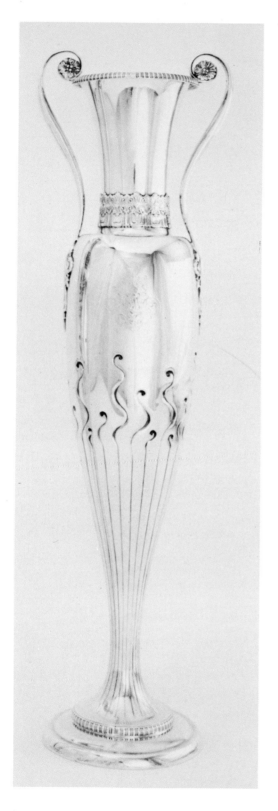

This book has been written for a specific purpose, and with a particular goal in mind. It is intended for the student and intelligent layman interested in American silver, its stylistic sequences, its formal development, and its aesthetic achievements. It attempts to give something of the history of this silver and its place in American life of the period. It is an object-oriented book; not so much an exhaustive survey as an effort to induce readers actually to look at the silver and discern its qualities of beauty as well as its historical associations.

Each chapter is arranged so that the dozen or so most important pieces from the period are discussed first, summarizing, as it were, the attainments of the particular style. The latter part of the chapter fills the picture in. In examining the range of silver surviving from the early periods, it is also possible to survey the careers of many of the major silversmiths and their places in society. In the later periods the increased numbers of craftsmen and their wares preclude such an approach. There I have tried to examine various individual and regional treatments of the general range of forms.

I have not tried to make this book a dictionary or encyclopedia, nor a series of definitive biographies of silversmiths. Stu-

Preface

dents in search of more extensive information about many of the objects here are referred to the catalogue of American silver in the Garvan and other collections at the Yale University Art Gallery, written by Kathryn C. Buhler and myself (Yale University Press, New Haven, Connecticut, 1970).

Virtually all the pieces illustrated here are from public collections where they are relatively accessible and available for study. If I seem to have used an unduly large number of illustrations from the Garvan Collection, the choice was dictated by the availability of good photographs.

Fine silver is beautiful. Studying it, understanding it, and contemplating it can lead not only to a greater awareness of the society that valued it, but also to a refined appreciation of form itself—with special reference, of course, to the kind of objects one uses and values in everyday life. If the silver can be handled, so much the better, for it was always meant to be; feeling the weight of it, turning it over in one's hand, catching the different reflections on its surface, and seeing the subtle variations in its bluish color are all an essential part of the experience of it.

My first debt is indubitably to my wife, without whose constant support and enthusiastic persuasion I would never have completed the book. Jules Prown had an important part in its inception, and to him I am deeply grateful. Willis Woods, Director of The Detroit Institute of Arts, with his customary warmth and fairness, made it possible for me to complete the writing of it. Frederick Cummings gave me invaluable moral support, and Wayne Andrews offered shrewd and perceptive comments. To Judy Beach I owe a special debt of gratitude, in that she gratuitously, and with excellent perception, made order out of the chaos of my initial manuscript. Margaret Ahlstrom helped enormously in the final stages of the book; Kyra Curtis and Betsy Gaidos were invaluable helpers, too. Brenda Gilchrist was very helpful in the initial stages of planning this book, and without Ellyn Childs the book would never have become a reality, for she kindly and ingeniously took care of innumerable details that are the birth pains of every book. I am very grateful to her.

Special thanks go to those kind people who helped me procure photographs, and information, particularly Margaret Stearns, Raymond Shepherd, Caroline Rollins, Heather Nary, Mary Glaze, Louisa Dresser, Elva McCormick, Henry Maynard, Ian Quimby, William de Matteo, and J. Herbert Gebelein.

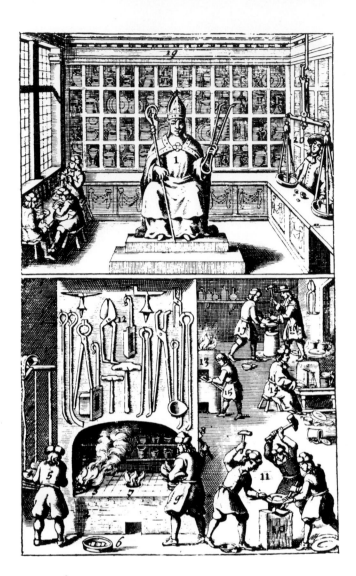

From William Badcock, *A New Touch-Stone for Gold and Silver Wares* (London, 1679).

1 *St.* Dunſtan, *the Patron of the* Goldſmiths *Company.*
2 *The Refining Furnace.*
3 *The* Teſt *with Silver refining on it.*
4 *The Fineing Bellows.*
5 *The Man blowing or working them.*
6 *The* Teſt *Mould.*
7 *A Wind-hole to melt Silver in without Bellows.*
8 *A pair of Organ Bellows.*
9 *A Man melting or Boiling, or nealing Sil-ver at them.*
10 *A Block, with a large Anvil placed thereon.*

11 *Three Men Forging Plate.*
12 *The Fineing and other Goldsmiths Tools.*
13 *The* Aſſay *Furnace.*
14 *The* Aſſay-Maſter *making* Aſſays.
15 *His Man putting the* Aſſays *into the Fire.*
16 *The Warden marking the Plate on the Anvil.*
17 *His Officer holding the Plate for the Marks.*
18 *Three Goldſmiths, ſmall-workers, at work.*
19 *A Goldſmiths Shop furniſhed with Plate.*
20 *A Goldſmith weighing Plate.*

CHAPTER ONE

Society, Silversmiths, and Their Wares

The demand for fine silversmiths and their wares existed primarily in urban societies. In the period from 1650 to 1900, the leading cities in America were Boston, New York, and Philadelphia. Accumulating great mercantile wealth, these cities became centers for a vigorous social and intellectual life. Most of the important and fine American silver of this period was ordered and made in these cities. They set the standards and established the patterns for subsidiary urban centers, such as Newport and Baltimore, which were also rich and cultured but which contributed little to the main stylistic trends of American silver. Southern society's preference for imported furnishings precluded its contributing much to the development of this native craft.

For most of this period, Boston, New York, and Philadelphia stood on a colonial periphery of the British Empire. Their mercantile and social connections with London were at least as frequent as with each other. The majority of their citizens —with the exception of the first settlers in New York—had immigrated from England, and until the Revolution, they were its citizens. By that time, the tradition of social dependence on the mother country was so deeply ingrained that in matters of taste and art England remained the paragon. Historically, colonial societies have always relied heavily on a strong center—such as Rome or Madrid—and America was no exception. So basic and powerful was this relationship with the capital, it easily overrode the multifarious influences that entered America through prolific trade, immigration, and the political incursions of rival colonial empires.

The leading settlers in America tried to establish and order society upon the models they had known in Europe, with the significant absence of a court and aristocracy. They had come from the rising middle classes of the Old World and their origins were always apparent, even when they formed a rich and powerful oligarchy, as in seventeenth-century Boston, or became wealthy landed gentry, as the patroons of early New York. For most of this period, society in these three main cities, despite its rapid growth and accumulation of wealth, consisted essentially of two classes, middle and lower, and this must be remembered in any study of its ideas and its tastes. Entirely foreign to the New World is the tradition of a European aristocracy, vastly endowed, mer-

11

curial in its fashions, and with a long tradition of imposing its own tastes and ideas on artists and craftsmen.

In these urban centers, founded upon English models and continually looking to London for guidance in intellectual and fashionable affairs, the rich inhabitants demanded silversmiths. Most of the settlers had brought all their wealth with them from the Old World. Expedience and long-established tradition dictated that this wealth was best transported in the form of silver objects or "plate" (as silver was generally called), rather than currency, with its fluctuations and infinite variations, or bulkier portables. Silver was precious, and, moreover, it was highly flexible; it could be quickly melted down and used as a form of currency to purchase goods and materials necessary to establish people in the New World. For this, and for the repair and maintenance of the plate they had brought with them, the settlers needed the services of silversmiths.

For these people, however, silver served a function beyond the merely pecuniary. Tradition, again, dictated that the amount of plate one possessed was a real and visible index to one's social standing, and in the New World from the beginning the settlers felt it necessary to establish and observe the modes of social behavior they had known in Europe, to convince themselves that their gamble was paying off. "I esteem it *as well politic as reputable,* to furnish myself with a handsome cupboard of plate," wrote an early settler, indicating the equal importance of the financial and the social functions of silver. This tradition lasted throughout our period in America. When the urban centers were well established, silver remained an essential part of a rich person's estate, more flexible and more easily handled than land, houses, and retainers, and more ostentatious (and also more easily identifiable) than specie.

As already observed, those who owned silver were the leaders of society and its rich citizens. Silver was a precious metal and therefore expensive (the price of silver at any given time means little without a full comprehension of the related prices of food, clothes, and land in proportion to a person's total wealth; but it is probably safe to say that a fine piece of silver cost as much as a significant art object for an individual today). Early inventories indicate that only about the top 5 per cent of society owned silver in any quantity. The silversmith, therefore, was used to dealing on an exclusive level. Indeed, the first American silversmiths inherited the tradition, medieval in origin but still alive in early-seventeenth-century England, of equality with (if not superiority to) any other artists or artisans in society. It was the Renaissance that broke this tradition and exalted the painter, the sculptor, and the architect above the silversmith, and the Renaissance cannot be said to have come to America, in all its ramifications, until the beginning of the eighteenth century. (In this respect, the arrival of the English painter John Smibert in 1729 serves as a focal point.) In addition to these social aspects, the early silversmith performed a useful service for rich citizens; since he needed a strong room, as fireproof as possible, for his own silver, he would often store others' silver too. Thus, he was frequently an extremely trustworthy and respected figure in society.

This period saw a great change in the social status of the silversmith, however. One of the earliest in Boston, John Hull, was a leader of his community; he became a successful silversmith and then used his abilities and his position to become a successful merchant also. He filled many of the necessary legal and social offices in the city, on a level with almost all his patrons. In the early history of the Bay Colony, he was a giant figure. After the first quarter of the eighteenth century no other silversmith in America even remotely resembled Hull in this respect. A useful comparison to reveal the silversmith's changed position is Paul Revere, also working in Boston, approximately a century later. Revere was one of Boston's two leading silversmiths, among many others of lesser quality, but here was a man willing to employ his manual dexterity in any direction, however insignificant—even to the making of false teeth. Yet it is not difficult to understand the change in Revere's attitude compared to his illustrious predecessor, for the circumstances were not propitious; even the finest artist in colonial America, John Singleton Copley, also working in Boston at this time, felt obliged to complain, "the people generally regard it [the art of painting] no more than any other useful trade, as they sometimes term it, like that of a carpenter, tailor or shewmaker." The next century saw an improvement in the social attitude to the artist and a corresponding decrease in the social role of the silversmith.

Those early settlers who brought silver with them appear to have brought mainly English silver of the late sixteenth and early seventeenth centuries, as well as silver from Holland and a little from other European countries. English silver seems to have been regarded as more highly desirable than American by certain elements in the three main cities throughout this period. There is frequent mention in early letters of whole services ordered from London to celebrate a special family event, even when several silversmiths of excellent quality were active in the same city. Silversmiths' advertisements frequently referred to imported silver as a standard that they tried to match.

Most of the objects brought by the early settlers were obviously of domestic type—not for everyday use, since they were so expensive, but mainly for ceremonial occasions, presumably. Tankards, cups, spoons, and dishes predominate, together with a whole range of specialized items such as holders for salt, sugar, or snuff. These were the forms that American silversmiths made also. Throughout this period new items necessitated by new social habits, such as the drinking of coffee and tea, appeared in England and were imported into America, largely replacing the ceremonial drinking vessels of the seventeenth century. In the nineteenth century, presentation pieces in the form of large pitchers and urns, previously unknown, appeared in increasing quantity. Many of these objects were fashioned to hold liquid. Since silver was not common, however, it is doubtful that their use was restricted to certain kinds of liquid—such as "caudle"—whose names have since been appended to certain forms; rather, they probably served a variety of purposes. Nomenclature can be confusing, since certain kinds of objects were given different names by different people at approximately the same time, and still other names later. To avoid confusion, the simplest, most descriptive terms, such as "two-handled cup," are used in this book.

In European countries, ecclesiastical silver for the Established churches often formed an important part of the output of silversmiths. Prescribed forms consisted generally of chalice and paten (or salver), flagon, and basin. The Nonconformist churches in Europe and America abolished the ritual surrounding Communion; instead of the priest alone handling the vessels, which were often consecrated, those partaking in the Communion passed vessels to each other. (The eighteenth-century engraving reproduced on p. 15 illustrates the practice.) In such instances, therefore, it was appropriate that these vessels should be of a normal domestic type, such as wine cups, two-handled cups, and tankards. A notable exception to this is the beaker, found in Nonconformist churches in Holland, southeast England, where contact with Holland was greatest, and in large quantities in New England. (This form was more common in Dutch than in English silver, although, in the seventeenth century, Dutch and English silver forms and styles were closely interrelated.) Its significant appearance in the New World was undoubtedly due to its religious uses. But such was the character of life in New England that it is impossible to say that the beaker was reserved solely for this. Many examples obviously saw long domestic service before being given to a church.

Many rich inhabitants of the New World followed the established European tradition of giving or bequeathing a silver Communion vessel to their church. A great many of these objects still exist, the early ones in particular having survived the vicissitudes of constant usage better than those that remained in private hands. Because of this, and the Nonconformist practice of inscribing the piece with the name of the donor and the date of the gift, and also the interchangeability of church and domestic forms, the corpus of silver in American churches forms an extremely valuable part of our study. The fact that a silver vessel was considered an appropriate—even handsome—gift to one's all-important place of worship (the spiritual connotations are undeniable) indicates the esteem in which these objects were held. The same might be said of objects not destined for the church; many were special gifts for significant occasions, such as christening, marriage, military victory.

The people who could afford a quantity of silver were often precisely those who took an absorbing interest in social and intellectual currents and in changing fashions. Here silver was again a valuable and flexible commodity, for an old-fashioned piece could be melted down and remade in the newest style. That is why the most successful silversmiths paid assiduous attention to the changing silver styles in England and incorporated new designs into their own work. As far as one can determine, the new styles appeared in America within a decade of their introduction in England. Since tastes and fashions die hard, it is obvious that the introduction of a new style did not mean the instantaneous disappearance of the old. This must be remembered in dating pieces of American silver.

As we have observed, the American patron of silversmiths was a particular kind of person, with a colonial's deference to the affairs of the mother country, involved in some way with the ubiquitous mercantile activity, and of the middle classes. These characteristics are reflected in the silver he acquired. It is virtually all—with the exception of New York silver before the second quarter of the eighteenth century—directly inspired by English domestic silver. The commonplace observation that American silver is plainer than English silver is based on the utterly fallacious comparison of American silver with the kind of English silver that was widely known earlier in this century—royal, aristocratic, ambassadorial. In general, Americans wanted the same as their English counterparts—the wealthy merchants of London and such rich provincial cities as Bristol, and the lesser landed gentry—fine forms, good weight, and strong surfaces. Any discussion of American silver must continually emphasize this profound dependence on English domestic silver styles and forms. Yet one of the inborn strengths of colonial society appeared also in its silver. The great distance of the American cities from London eliminated the continual weakening of their society by the movement of the most ambitious and talented elements to the capital—the center of activities. This was a major problem for provincial cities in England. Thus, large provincial centers in

14

Communion in a Nonconformist Church. From Jean Frédéric Bernard. *Cérémonies et coutumes religieuses de tous les peuples du monde* (Amsterdam, 1723). Rare Book Division, The New York Public Library; Astor, Lenox and Tilden Foundations.

America developed strong local characteristics. These regional characteristics or variations appeared in, and help to distinguish, the decorative arts of Boston, New York, and Philadelphia in a way that is not so apparent in the decorative arts of England.

Silversmiths in England all belonged to a rich and powerful guild that, at the time of the settlement of America, had functioned for more than five hundred years. The guild carefully regulated the practices and behavior of its members. Al-

though it did not extend its authority to the American colonies, a tradition of scrupulousness appears to have been largely inherent in the craft, for, even without guild control, silversmiths in America were mainly conscientious in their practices and attitudes. Even the absence in America of the English governmental assay mark (to establish the quantity of pure silver in the object) does not appear to have resulted in wares of debased content. Misdemeanors, such as short-changing or counterfeiting the currency that silversmiths handled so often,

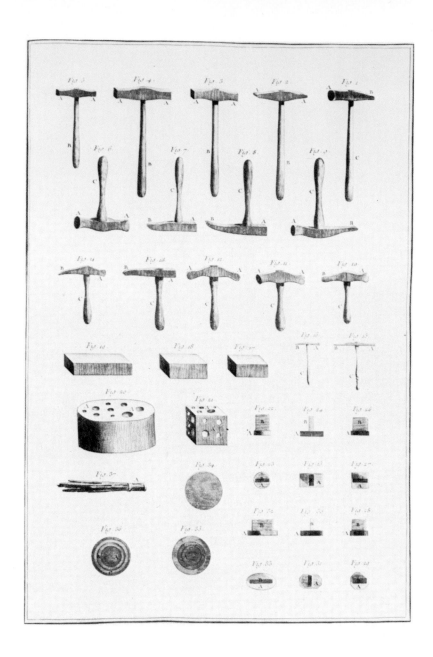

Tools of the silversmith—hammers, dies, anvils, stakes, and swages. From Denis Diderot, ed., *Encyclopédie, Dictionnaire des Sciences* (Paris, 1771). General Research and Humanities Division, The New York Public Library; Astor, Lenox and Tilden Foundations.

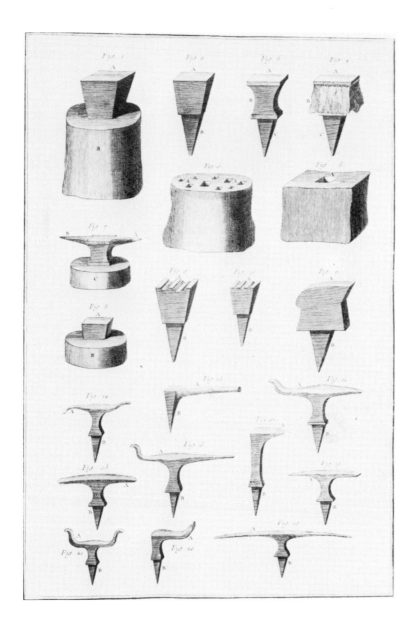

were quickly dealt with by the civil authorities.

In England and its colonies in the seventeenth and eighteenth centuries, the established—if not the only—method of entering a craft profession was through the apprentice system. This was intended to supplement formal education, as well as to introduce the young to the theory and practices of the craft. As the system was an indissoluble part of European society, it was quickly established by civil ordinance in the three main cities in America. If children from all but the richer families started some kind of manual work at about the age of three, it must be expected that a young man was considered ready to learn an adult profession by the age of fourteen. As an apprentice, he was bound to a silversmith by indenture; the master agreed to teach him the "art and mystery" of the craft and keep, feed, and clothe him in return for his labor. A silversmith could take in several apprentices, so he probably organized his shop's activity to a large extent on their labor and progressive skill. Apprentices were bound to their master for a period of at least seven years, and were not allowed to open their own businesses until they were twenty-one years of age. By that time, presumably, they were skilled and well trained in the careful handling of precious metals and, therefore, of considerable sums of money. At that time, they would need capital to acquire the many special tools necessary in this craft, as well as to accumulate a stock of silver.

An established silversmith would have in stock many of the smaller, staple objects such as spoons and porringers, buckles, and other personal items. It seems likely that only the largest pieces, such as flagons and two-handled cups or, from the end of the eighteenth century, waiters or trays, tea and coffee services, requiring a considerable outlay of silver, were invariably commissioned. The silversmith probably kept a supply of all the smaller objects ready for immediate sale or for engraving with the purchaser's initials or arms. Many silversmiths also kept a stock of silver, jewelry, and gewgaws imported from Europe. (The cabinet in the picture of the silversmith's shop, p. 10, contained ready-made items of this sort.)

To make an object such as a flagon (see Fig. 75) or coffeepot, the silversmith would first need the requisite number of silver coins to melt down, to alloy (the English or sterling standard was 92.5 per cent silver, with 7.5 per cent copper added for hardness), and cast into ingots; or an old piece of silverware; or the raw material itself. Although important silver mines were not discovered in North America until the mid-nineteenth century, the Spanish colony of Mexico was, of course, fabulously rich in silver (which made

Spanish vessels returning from Mexico such alluring targets for American privateers). The silversmith would hammer an ingot, or a part of one, into a flat sheet approximately one quarter of an inch thick. With compasses or scriber he would then mark a circle on this sheet, cut it out, and start hammering the disk with a ball-headed hammer on an anvil. This would have the effect of raising up the edges of the disk, so that by constant hammering and manipulation the silversmith would create a cup or rounded-cone shape. With different shaped hammers (he would probably own more than a hundred) on different shaped anvils (he may have had over fifty of these), the silversmith would create the long, almost cylindrical body of the flagon. Since repeated hammering makes silver brittle, the silversmith would continually anneal the metal by heating it red hot and plunging it into a bath of water and sulphuric acid. This would soften the silver and make it more malleable while also dissolving the surface copper to leave a layer of pure white silver on the surface. It needed, of course, considerable skill to maintain a constant thickness up the wall of the vessel. When finished with the heavy hammers, the silversmith would take a planishing hammer —lighter, and with a highly polished surface—to smooth out any irregularities in the surface of the vessel. Another method of making such a body, especially popular in later periods because of the wider availability of sheet silver, was seaming. The silversmith would gently hammer or bend a sheet into a tube shape, then solder the long vertical seam.

Moldings for the lip and base of the hollow body were generally made by pulling (or "drawing") strips of silver through a shaped aperture. These were then joined to the body with silver solder. The cover of the vessel was probably hammered (or "raised") also, but, by the middle of the eighteenth century, may have been cast;

18

the mold for this was made from specially prepared sand and a wood, brass, or silver template. Thumbpiece, hinge plate, and finial were cast, while the handle was generally raised in two pieces and soldered (or, in the case of tea and coffeepots, carved from fruit wood). The whole would then be soldered together, heated, and burnished with pumice stone or other fine abrasive to hide solder marks and bring out the full luster of the metal, and made ready for surface decoration—engraving or chasing.

Busy silversmiths, particularly in the later periods, employed skilled workmen especially for engraving or chasing, although these were a necessary part of their own skills. Engraving consisted of gouging a linear design from the surface of the silver—arms, cartouches or mantling (derived, in their successive styles, from English books on heraldry or directly from English silver), or initials. Chasing ("repoussé" or "embossing") displaced silver on the surface but did not remove it. First, the vessel was filled with hard but resilient pitch, and details of the design impressed from the front with the use of specially shaped punches and a hammer. Simple linear designs (see Fig. 13) would be chased or "flat-chased" from the front, while more ambitious designs (see Fig. 12) would be effected from front and back. On vessels with narrow apertures the design was effected totally from the front, then pushed out from the inside when the pitch was melted away. The design was thus in relief on the face of the vessel and also apparent in reverse on the back or inside. After the final polishing, the silversmith generally (but not invariably) stamped the piece with his tiny mark—in the early period his initials, and in later periods his full name. He was not obliged, as he would have been in England, to have it inspected at a local assay office, where it would be stamped with a letter indicating the date, a device indicating the city of origin, and the guarantee of silver content.*

Silversmiths charged their customers for the weight of silver in each piece as well as for the amount of labor involved. An elaborately chased or engraved piece would obviously cost more than a plain object because of the extra work put into it. If the customer had brought silver to the craftsman in the form of coins or an old piece, this would be weighed and deducted from the cost of the new piece. Some idea of the charges involved can be derived from the calculation of one silversmith around 1760 that it took ten working days to make a plain coffeepot (such as Fig. 148) before the addition of any decoration.

Throughout our period, silversmiths in England far outnumbered those active in the colonies, while English silver retained an allure for fashionable society in America. Consequently, the amount of silver known to have been made in America is small in comparison to that made in England. Furthermore, information on the origin of American pieces is nebulous compared to English silver, as the discussion of methods of marking silver suggests. But the rarity of American silver and the amount of judicious investigation required to establish its origins and dates are part of its continual fascination. American silversmiths' strong dependence on English forms should not overshadow the fact that these objects were made by the skill of the hand and the judgment of the eye, and that a beautiful, vital form is always worthy of study and contemplation.

* From 1814 to 1830, Baltimore silver was assayed, dated, and stamped. The word *Standard* is sometimes found on silver of the 1830's, indicating that it contained the quantity of pure silver—89.2 per cent—found in silver coinage in America from 1792 until 1837. In that year, the standard was changed by government legislation to 90 per cent. *Pure Coin* or *Coin* or the letters D and C were also used after 1850. From 1865, legislation enforced the use of the word *Sterling* for the same silver standard.

CHAPTER TWO

The Seventeenth Century

1

America in the sevententh century offers a fascinating picture of embryonic settlements developing into established cities with flourishing intellectual lives in the short span of sixty years. Within this context of a rather transparent fabric of society is an exceptional opportunity to study the silversmith at work. No other period of American silversmithing is so easily circumscribed, given the small number of silversmiths and the limited amount of silver that has survived; only in Boston and New York was there any appreciable amount of silversmithing in the seventeenth century. Yet no other period shows such diverse stylistic influences. Some of the finest and boldest silver ever made in America was created at this time.

Seventeenth-century styles were patterned closely after the Puritan (or Commonwealth) and Restoration styles in England, and contemporary Dutch silver.

Subsequent, fully developed Baroque forms began to appear in the 1690's. Boston was then a wealthy, thriving city of about seven thousand inhabitants. The increasing number of rich merchants there challenged the supremacy of the clerical oligarchy and had an undeniable effect on the tone and color of society. By the last years of the century, Boston's richer citizens had enjoyed for well over a decade one or more coffee

2

1. Beaker, *ca.* 1659, by John Hull and Robert Sanderson; H. 3⅞ inches. First and Second Church, Boston. Photograph courtesy of Museum of Fine Arts, Boston.

2. Dram cup, *ca.* 1650–60, by John Hull and Robert Sanderson; H. 1½ inches. Yale University Art Gallery, New Haven, Connecticut. The Mabel Brady Garvan Collection.

---

houses, private and public coaches, a public library, printing presses and almost two dozen bookshops, French dancing masters, and relief from sumptuary laws prohibiting "the brilliant plumage" of fancy clothes, lace, gold braid, and slashed sleeves. No other provincial city in the British Empire had garnered such wealth, and none was more intellectually active.

New York was probably the most cosmopolitan city in America in this period. Dutch influence was still paramount there by the end of the century, although thirty years of British rule had obviously offset this influence somewhat. The end of the period saw a considerable influx of French Huguenot immigrants. With only four thousand inhabitants, New York was not so rich as Boston, while the internal conflict of the Dutch and English impaired its intellectual and social development.

Into these two cities in the seventeenth century poured wealth from trade and immigration. Currencies were of a truly international character. In an effort to stabilize the situation, the Bay Colony established its own mint in Boston in 1652. This lasted until the end of the century, with only limited success. By the 1670's, the importation of Spanish coin into Boston was so large that efforts were made to get it accepted as part of the regular currency. Most of the currency in New

York during the latter part of the century appears to have been Spanish. All currencies of that time had, of course, a very high silver content.

Immigration enriched the cities enormously, not only in the obvious way of talent and manpower but also by the transmission of personal wealth. "The four grand settlements of New England," wrote the eighteenth-century historian Daniel Neal, "beside the loss of so many inhabitants, cost the Kingdom of England no less than 4 or 500,000 pounds, a vast sum of money at that time." Neal believed that, if the persecution of the Puritans in England in the seventeenth century had continued for another decade or two, "a fourth part of the riches of the Kingdom would have been carried out of it." The most easily transportable form of this wealth, silver plate, was mainly of English and Dutch origin, although contemporary inventories indicate that French, Spanish, and Portuguese silver was not uncommon.

Silversmiths were essential in these rapidly expanding societies. The first one recorded in Massachusetts appeared only a few years after the landing of the Pilgrims—John Mansfield, in Charlestown in 1634 By 1680, Boston supported· twenty-four silversmiths. Most of the older men had served their apprenticeships in London, but by that date they themselves had trained a group of native-born craftsmen. Boston became a microcosm of London, in the sense that it fulfilled the role of silversmithing center for the whole of its surrounding area. It completely overshadowed New York in this respect, even in the southeastern areas of New England closest to that city. Prior to the Revolution, only eighteen pieces of silver by four New York makers found their way into the New England churches, compared to the hundreds of Boston-made pieces. The well-known Van Rensselaer family of New York even apprenticed one of its sons,

Kiliaen, to a Boston silversmith rather than to a New York craftsman, in the 1680's. Boston silversmiths never formed any organization to enforce their predominance (although many of them signed the "handycraftsmen's" petition to the General Court in 1677 seeking trade protection). A reputation for quality, honesty, and being *au courant* with the latest fashions served to establish and maintain their prominence.

Compared to the Boston silversmiths, most of whom had English origins or anglicized names, the New York silversmiths by the 1690's were all of Dutch or French extraction. There were only half as many active in New York as in Boston. They made much of the silver that remains from the period for the Reformed Dutch churches of New York and New Jersey, as the Boston silversmiths made much of the surviving seventeenth-century New England silver for the Nonconformist churches there.

Most of the English silver that the earliest settlers brought with them was Elizabethan or Jacobean in style; certain of these pieces were given to the Boston churches later on. It was natural that the so-called "Puritan" or plain style, popular in English domestic silver in the first half of the seventeenth century, should find favor in New England, and inevitable that it should remain the dominant style throughout this period. Although elaborate styles—now Baroque—returned to England with the restoration of Charles II, it appears that plain styles were popular with certain segments of society throughout the century, as they were in New England.

Any discussion of major pieces of silver from any of the style periods should begin with dated pieces—but a word of caution is necessary here. It has already been pointed out that the American silversmith was not legally required to have his wares stamped with marks indicating sterling content and place and time of origin (he was not even obliged to stamp his own mark on them, and occasionally did not). However, he frequently engraved the initials of early owners on the more important items, usually in a triangular pattern, with the first initials of husband and wife at the bottom and the first initial of their surname at the apex. A tradition has grown up that an object so marked was a wedding gift, and that it is datable to the time of the marriage. This method of dating is utterly unreliable. Occasionally a piece with such initials is accompanied by a date; but even here caution should be exercised, since the date might have been added later, and, even if it is contemporary with the initials, there is no absolute guarantee that the object was new when the engraving was added.

Church silver can provide useful information for dating various forms and motifs, since many of the pieces bear dates and initials, and church records frequently provide supplementary evidence about the gift. But the situation is still complicated. There is no guarantee that a church immediately bought a piece of silver after a particular gift or bequest of money. Many years might elapse between the gift and the purchase, although when an object was acquired it might be engraved with the date of the original gift. Even if an object was bought immediately after a gift, it might not be new. Silver was always valuable, and some pieces were given or acquired by churches a century after they were made. Although pieces given to a church during the donor's lifetime are the most reliably dated, they may still have been bought new and used privately for a decade or so before entering the church's possession, being marked then with the date of the gift.

Many factors should be considered in dating pieces. Maker, style, and ownership should all be taken into account first.

Obviously, important, expensive presentation pieces, either for church or private use, may be considered contemporary with any dates engraved on them, since it is unlikely that they would be old silver or that the maker would carry such important pieces in stock.

One of the earliest dated pieces of American silver is a small beaker bearing the pricked letters "T/BC" (for The Boston Church or the First Church, founded in 1630), and the date 1659 (Fig. 1). Surpassingly simple in design, it has a short, cylindrical body with a slightly flared lip. Decoration is restricted to a wide band of punched or "matted" ornamentation of a kind popular in England since the beginning of the seventeenth century. A simple shield serves as a reserve for the lettering and the date. In its appearance of pure functionalism and with its restrained decoration it seems to exemplify the Puritan mode. The beaker bears the marks of John Hull (1624–83) and Robert Sanderson (1608–93), who were master and partner respectively of the Massachusetts Mint, and undoubtedly the leading silversmiths in Boston at this time.

There is no reason to believe that the date the beaker bears is not approximately the date of its manufacture. Another object probably made in the same decade is a dram cup, or small two-handled cup, also by Hull and Sanderson (Fig. 2). On the basis of engraved initials added to this cup, it has been dated 1651. This evidence is unreliable, but it is certainly among the earliest pieces of American silver. Intended for the service of wine or spirits, the cup is a little more elaborately decorated than the beaker. A line of punched dots rings the lip and the bottom of the bowl above the stepped base, flat-chased double lines divide the sides between the handles into panels, and crude, flat-chased floral designs are placed in each panel. On the bottom is flat-chased

Capt. Willets donation to
y Ch. of Rehoboth 1674

3

4

3. Standing cup, *ca.* 1674, by John Hull and Robert Sanderson; H. 7⅜₆ inches. Yale University Art Gallery, New Haven, Connecticut. The Mabel Brady Garvan Collection.

4. Tankard, *ca.* 1676, by Jeremiah Dummer; H. 6⅜₆ inches. Courtesy of The Henry Francis du Pont Winterthur Museum, Winterthur, Delaware.

a Tudor rose. Two twisted wire handles in scroll-shape give a feeling of grace and elevation to what otherwise appears (as with the beaker) a very earth-bound object. If the decoration is crude, it is also a characteristic of English silver of this period; indeed, this type of ornamentation has been described by an authority on English silver as apparently executed by a child with a blunt nail. A similar design, carved against a background of the same kind of punched decoration seen on the beaker, can be found on English and American furniture of the seventeenth century.

Perhaps the loveliest piece of silver from this period is the standing cup by Hull and Sanderson, given to the Congregational Church in Rehoboth (which is now East Providence, Rhode Island) about 1674 *(Fig. 3)*. Like so many objects from this period it was used for both domestic and church purposes, being called variously a wine cup, church cup, and bowl. It may have been made up to a decade before it entered the church's possession; of the nine known examples of this form by Hull and Sanderson that have survived, four were used domestically for many years before being given to churches.

What makes this standing cup so superb in design is the successful blending of the strength and solidity of cup and broad foot and the elegant drawing of the knopped stem. In units of measurement it utilizes the four-to-three variant: Diameter and height of cup and diameter of foot are all four units, while the height of the stem is three units. Since the stem is narrower, it is made proportionately shorter, to emphasize the aspect of strength. Derived in form from the Elizabethan and Jacobean "steeple" cups (the term denotes the tall cover)—a fine example of which was brought to Boston at an early date and given to the First Church—and closely resembling the chalices of the

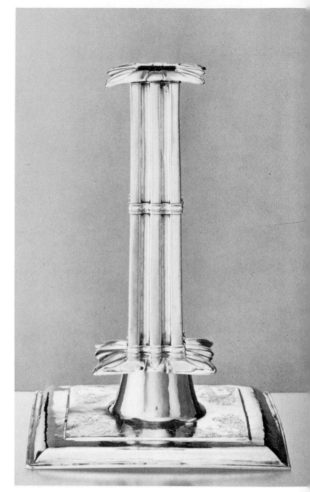

5

5. Candlestick (one of a pair), *ca.* 1680–90, by Jeremiah Dummer; H. 10¹³⁄₁₆ inches. Yale University Art Gallery, New Haven, Connecticut. The Mabel Brady Garvan Collection.

6. Two-handled covered cup, *ca.* 1680–90, by John Coney; H. 6¹¹⁄₁₆ inches. Yale University Art Gallery, New Haven, Connecticut. The Mabel Brady Garvan Collection.

6

Established Church, this type of cup found great favor in seventeenth-century New England.

Hull and Sanderson's first native-born apprentice, by whom any appreciable amount of silver survives, was Jeremiah Dummer (1645–1718). He made two superb early tankards for the church in Charlestown, Massachusetts, which were bought with a bequest of 1676. These pieces, one of which is illustrated here *(Fig. 4)*, are among the masterpieces of New England seventeenth-century silver. The broad, tapered drum of the body, the

graceful wide, low cover, and the double-cupped thumbpiece (recalling the curve of the handle in miniature) suggest a date of manufacture in the last two or three decades of the century. Complementing this are such details as the low, simple molding at the base of the body, the long V-shaped drop at the upper juncture of handle and body, the V-shaped drop on the handle below the hinge, and the shape of the handle end (or terminal)—here a simple shield with a projecting serration above. The proportions of body width to height are square over all *(see Fig. 1)*, giving the impression of great strength and solidity. More apparent in this piece than in the Hull and Sanderson cup *(see Fig. 3)*, but a marked characteristic of plain silver of this period, is the very evident "rippling" aspect of the surface. This intentional effect derives from the hammering of the body, and it creates subtle patterns as light moves over the surface. It is even more apparent in the later cup by John Coney *(see Fig. 6)*. For such a purpose, but more obvious, seventeenth-century furniture was relief-carved and painted.

Only one pair of American candlesticks has survived from this period *(Fig. 5)*. Magnificent and bold in form, they were also made by Jeremiah Dummer. Of a cluster-columned or fluted design, the square shaft is set on a square base, with a round, splayed stem making the transition between them. In a primarily vertical design there are horizontal accents at the foot, and at the bottom, middle, and top of the shaft. Proportionately, there are three vertical units of measurement and two horizontal units (obviously a simple variation on the four-to-three proportion). The candlesticks appear to have been made in the 1680's: The earliest of four coats-of-arms on the foot is engraved in the style of that decade. The superlative design and execution of these candlesticks

7. Two-handled cup, *ca.* 1685–95, by John Coney; H. 5 inches. Harvard University, Cambridge, Massachusetts.

7

do not suffer in comparison with similar forms found in England Holland, and France in the seventeenth century made of silver, enamel, pewter, and brass. Their form has also been compared to the architectural details of cluster-columned chimneys, still surviving on some seventeenth-century New England houses. Forms such as these were part of the general vocabulary of style of the period, used throughout the range of decorative arts. Designs such as that on the stem of the standing cup, for example *(see Fig. 3)*, can be found cut into maple members of contemporary New England furniture.

A decade younger than Dummer but in all probability trained by the same masters, John Coney (1656–1722) is the third great New England silversmith of the seventeenth century. His monumental two-handled covered cup *(Fig. 6)* is the only example of the form known to have survived from New England of that period, although it is not uncommon in contemporary English silver. Standing on a stepped bottom similar to that of the dram cup *(see Fig. 2)*, the cup has a broad belly and wide neck. The simple overlapping cover has a trumpet-shaped handle that also serves as a foot when the cover is inverted, changing it into a convenient salver or stand. Of elaborate scroll shape, the beaded caryatid handles are cast (the most common method for making handles for such cups in the seventeenth century). The final rich embellishment is the Addington arms engraved on the side of the vessel, within a beautifully executed, late-seventeenth-century cartouche. Standing about six and three-quarters inches high, this heavy cup weighs more than thirty-one ounces; by comparison, the Dummer candlestick is about ten and three-quarters inches high and weighs twenty-five ounces. Very apparent here is the rippling-surface effect previously mentioned. Measuring two units high and three wide, the cup has the appearance of grandness and massiveness. Despite the scrolled movement of the handles and the engraving, it sits very solidly on its base. Because of its close formal relationship to other Coney two-handled cups (without covers) of the 1680's, it is safe to say that this example dates from that decade.

Similar in form, Coney's later two-handled cup *(Fig. 7)* is ornamented with an exemplary seventeenth-century type of decoration. Enormously popular in England after the Restoration (it was actually derived from Dutch silver), this decoration of naturalistic forms proliferating over the surface of the piece is found on New England silver in the last two decades of the century. It tends to increase the boldness and heavy appearance of the forms. In its rather weighty exuberance it signifies the emergence of Baroque styles in the New World.

One of the finest and tallest of all New England beakers was made by John Coney for the First Congregational Church of Ipswich, Massachusetts *(Fig. 8)*. It probably dates from the last decade of the century. Bought with a bequest from Thomas Knoulton, it bears simply his engraved name. Proportionately three units high and two wide, the beaker has an undeniable grandeur. The slight surface movement, the low base molding, the accentuated flare of the body (uncommon in a New England beaker of this date), and the straightforward inscription all contribute to a controlled simplicity characteristic of the best seventeenth-century silver.

Dwarfing even this tall beaker is the first New York piece discussed here, made by Cornelius van der Burch (*ca.* 1653-99), and engraved with the name of Robbert Sandersen and the date 1685 *(Fig. 9)*. It stands eight inches high and is a little more than half that width. Its elaborate engraved decoration and its complex base molding make it one of the richest and grandest objects in all American silver of

8

the seventeenth century. The engraved flowers and scrolled foliage within interlaced strapwork at the lip, and the crossed branches forming reserves on the sides, are derived from sixteenth-century Dutch designs. Similar decoration appears on several New York beakers of this period, although the reserves are more usually seen on church beakers enclosing symbols of Faith, Hope, and Charity. The form of the base molding is also derived from Dutch prototypes. Here the squared design is stamped while the scalloping at the top edge of the molding is cut. The strong rim of the base provides substantial visual support for this large object. Apart from its size, what makes this beaker so important is the unusual feature of engraved

pictorial scenes derived from illustrations by the Dutch artist Adrian van der Venne (1589–1662) for the collected works of Jacobus Cats (1577–1660). An edition of Cats's works was published in Amsterdam in 1655. On this beaker the foliate oval reserves contain symbols of Virtue, Industry, and Integrity, while the scenes at the base are intended to give lessons in Magnanimity (the spider being caught by the lizard, being caught by the stork, being caught by the snake, being caught by the hunters), Humility (a tortoise, delighted by the new dimension of flight, but held aloft by an eagle and about to be dropped on a rock), and Faithfulness (a crocodile continuing to grow, even in the presence of death). Obviously wholly

9

8. Beaker, *ca.* 1692, by John Coney; H. 6¾ inches. Yale University Art Gallery, New Haven, Connecticut. The Mabel Brady Garvan Collection.

9. Beaker, *ca.* 1685, by Cornelius van der Burch; H. 8 inches. Yale University Art Gallery, New Haven, Connecticut. The Mabel Brady Garvan Collection.

10

10. Tankard, *ca.* 1690–1700, by Jacobus van der Spiegel, H. 7¹¹⁄₁₆ inches. Yale University Art Gallery, New Haven, Connecticut. Gift of Spotswood D. Bowers and Mr. and Mrs. Francis P. Garvan.

indebted to Dutch models, this beaker has superb proportions and a commanding presence.

Elaborate, extensive engraved decoration was inherent in the Dutch tradition of seventeenth-century New York silversmithing. It imparts to the best of these objects a special distinction. Such is the quality of the tankard *(Fig. 10)* by Jacobus van der Spiegel (1668–1708). Dating probably from the last years of the century, as its broad drum indicates, it nevertheless utilizes elements that are later in style than those of the Dummer tankard *(see Fig. 4)*. The cover is higher and the dome is squarer in profile (a similar change occurred in later New England tankards); the base molding is higher and more elaborate; and the thumbpiece is now a corkscrew form. The long V-shaped drop on the body below the upper handle juncture is no longer employed, while a small, cast relief ornament in the form of a *lion couchant* has been applied to the top of the handle below the hinge—a feature that becomes a characteristic of New York silver. On the handle terminal (now disk-shaped) is applied another cast ornament in the form of a cherub's head; such heads were sometimes applied to New England tankard thumbpieces around the turn of the century. Also typical of New York is the stamped, repeated ornament at the baseband, here also enriched by a line of applied meander-wire. Although the engraved cartouche around the arms on the front of the tankard is similar in design to that of the Coney two-handled covered cup, it is tighter and more vigorous. (The swags of fruit under the shield are of Dutch derivation and also become a characteristic of New York silver.) Tightly swirled in the Dutch manner, superbly rhythmical and beautifully executed, the engraved decoration raises this tankard to the status of a masterpiece.

Again characteristic of New York, and again derived from Dutch prototypes, is the two-handled paneled bowl by Cornelius Kierstede (1675–1757), probably the most magnificent example of this form *(Fig. 11)*. Approximately hemispherical in shape, the body is articulated by chased vertical lines that divide the sides into panels, and, within each panel, a chased scrolled outline that forms a reserve. Within the reserve is chased a bold, intricately detailed flower, masterful in execution. On the bottom of the bowl is another flower in relief. Slightly raised on a foot that has a band of the stamped, repeated ornament we have come to expect on New York silver of this time, the bowl has two cast, beaded caryatid handles of the type already seen on the Coney two-handled covered cup *(see Fig. 6)*. Again massive and solid in appearance, befitting the period of its creation, the bowl is given internal rhythms and a feeling of subtle movement by the decoration on the handles, foot, and particularly the sides. In the bold symmetry of the panels and flowers, however, it prefigures the Baroque William and Mary styles.

The same may be said of the two-handled covered cup *(Fig. 12)* by Gerrit Onckelbag (*ca.* 1670–1732). Although completely English in appearance, this type of cup survives in the colonies only from New York; three examples are known. The symmetrical foliage on the body and cover is a precursor to the regular geometrical ornament widely used in the ensuing William and Mary period. It also becomes a developed characteristic of furniture of this time. The geometrical version of the caryatid handles, and the raised foot (later than the stepped bottom of the Coney piece), suggest a date in the last decade of the century. Indicative of this date also is the splendid cartouche surrounding the Bayard arms, which is similar to that on the Van der Spiegel tankard *(see Fig. 10)*. The seventeenth-century practice of making the cover double as a stand reappears; instead

11

11. Two-handled bowl, *ca.* 1690–1710, by Cornelius Kierstede; H. 4½ inches. The Metropolitan Museum of Art, New York. Lee Fund, 1938.

12. Two-handled covered cup, *ca.* 1690–1700, by Gerrit Onckelbag; H. 5¾ inches. Yale University Art Gallery, New Haven, Connecticut. The Mabel Brady Garvan Collection.

12

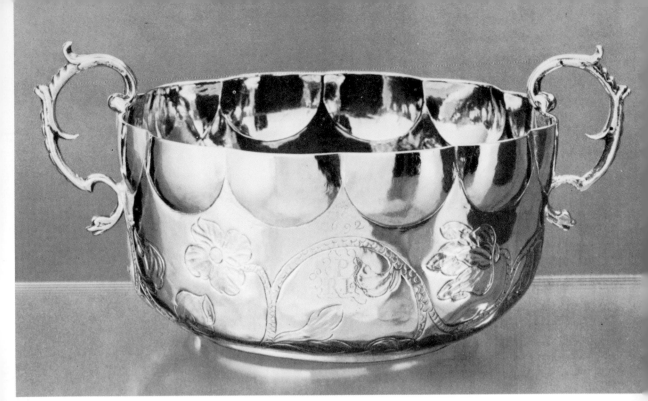

13

13. Two-handled bowl, *ca.* 1690–1700, by Jeremiah Dummer; H. 4⅜ inches. Yale University Art Gallery, New Haven, Connecticut. The Mabel Brady Garvan Collection.
14. Standing cup, *ca.* 1674, by John Hull and Robert Sanderson; H. 8¼ inches. First and Second Church, Boston. Photograph courtesy of Museum of Fine Arts, Boston.

of the single handle that Coney employed *(see Fig. 6)*, Onckelbag here placed three scroll brackets. This cup retains exactly the same proportional measurements as the Coney cup, three units wide to two high, despite the fact that it stands on a raised foot. The development from this primarily horizontal aspect can be seen in the following period.

The last decade of the century witnessed a mingling of the waning Puritan or plain styles and the waxing Baroque styles. Evidence of this can be found in the previous three objects. In a sense it can be found in the unique two-handled bowl by Jeremiah Dummer *(Fig. 13)*, although this illustration may be somewhat misleading, since the bowl seems to be patterned after Iberian seventeenth-century prototypes. Plunder from Spanish treasure ships entering Boston through privateer (or piratical) activities was the likely source for such a prototype. Yet the regularity of the lobed ornamentation at

the lip is fully Baroque in feeling. The same effect, on a broader scale, is given by the regularly indented rim of the Kierstede bowl *(see Fig. 11)*. Dummer retained the early type of stepped bottom for this piece, while the cast handles (with snake's-head terminals) are obviously variants of the early caryatid type. As a further embellishment and a counterpoint (not entirely successful) to the pronounced geometrical ornament, Dummer added asymmetrical, naturalistic flat-chasing, in the manner of the Coney cup

14

(*see Fig. 7*) but shallow in depth and more fluid in rhythm. This piece also dates from the last decade of the century.

John Hull and Robert Sanderson are the key figures in Boston silversmithing of the seventeenth century, for they made most of the earliest surviving silver and trained the finest silversmiths of the following generation. Hull was born in England in 1624 and received instruction in Boston from his half-brother, Richard Storer. (Storer had been trained by a London silversmith but had not completed his apprenticeship before his family emigrated; he may not have practiced the craft to any great extent in Boston.) Only one piece with Hull's mark alone has survived—a beaker similar to the example in the First Church dated 1659 (*see Fig. 1*), although somewhat more tapered. Presumably he practiced as a silversmith for only a few years before he was appointed Master of the Massachusetts Mint in 1652.

At that time, he chose for his partner Robert Sanderson, who had been an active silversmith in London before his emigration in the late 1630's. A few pieces marked by Sanderson alone are known, most of them presumably made after Hull's death in 1683. Since Hull was deeply involved with the mint and other commercial interests, it has been conjectured that Sanderson was the active silversmith of the partnership. Yet most of the approximately three dozen objects by the two men that are known today bear both marks.

In addition to his success with silversmithing and his merchant's acumen, Hull was noted as a public servant. He was a selectman and treasurer of the town of Boston, subsequently treasurer of the Colony, and also captain of the Artillery Company. He was one of the founders of the Third Church in Boston, established in 1669. His diaries and letters give carefully detailed accounts of his life and his

15

cups *(Fig. 14)* purchased by the First Church, Boston, with a bequest from John Oxenbridge (*d.* 1674). These appear more massive than the Rehoboth cup, with a broader, heavier bowl and a cylindrical stem with a single heavy knop. While these pieces convey a great deal of bold vigor, they are not nearly so finely proportioned nor so successfully integrated as the Rehoboth piece. It is a short step from the design of the Rehoboth cup to the fully developed baluster stem of the remaining Hull and Sanderson cups (in the First Church, Quincy, Massachusetts), a design that was also utilized in the following period by the silversmiths Hull and Sanderson had trained *(see Fig. 46).*

Apart from this type of small beaker, both plain and with punched decoration, Hull and Sanderson also made large beakers. Two of these have survived. They are both close to Dutch examples of the early seventeenth century; indeed, an almost identical Amsterdam beaker, made in 1637, probably belonged to Sanderson and subsequently became the property of the First Church, Boston. Both the large Hull and Sanderson beakers were used privately for about a hundred years before being given to churches. The one illustrated here *(Fig. 15)* utilizes a more typically seventeenth-century baseband than the other example (now in the Yale University Art Gallery). With stamped, repeated ornamentation, slight, splayed foot, and engraved, intertwined strapwork, it is also close to Dutch-inspired New York examples. It is a handsome form, with the flared mouth repeating, on an expanded scale, the outward movement of the base.

Several small two-handled cups by the partners are decorated with primitive flat-chased designs, such as those seen in Figure 2. The cup in the First Church of Dorchester, Massachusetts, is probably the earliest of the three illustrated here *(Fig. 16).* Compared to the cup in Figure 18, which is by Sanderson alone and typi-

business—he traded in everything, it appears, from horses to haberdashery. From these documents emerges a picture of a good Puritan but a rather unpleasant man. About Sanderson nothing of consequence is known.

The most important pieces by Hull and Sanderson that have survived are nine standing cups, one of which has already been discussed *(see Fig. 3).* Slightly earlier in style, in all probability, is a set of three

16

17

15. Beaker, *ca.* 1660–80, by John Hull and Robert Sanderson; H. 6 inches. Formerly First Congregational Church, Marblehead, Massachusetts. Photograph courtesy of Yale University Art Gallery, New Haven, Connecticut.

16. Two-handled cup, *ca.* 1660–80, by John Hull and Robert Sanderson; H. 3 inches. Second Church, Dorchester, Massachusetts. Photograph courtesy of Museum of Fine Arts, Boston.

17. Two-handled cup, *ca.* 1670–85, by John Hull and Robert Sanderson; H. 3$\frac{3}{16}$ inches. Courtesy of Museum of Fine Arts, Boston. Spalding Collection.

18. Two-handled cup, *ca.* 1670–85, by Robert Sanderson; H. 3⅝ inches. First and Second Church, Boston. Photograph courtesy of Museum of Fine Arts, Boston.

18

cal of the forms of the 1680's, the curves of the belly of the Dorchester cup are less accentuated, and the neck is almost as wide as the body. The small geometrical forms of the handles repeat the geometrical elements of the flat-chased decoration. Almost archaic in quality are the flowers or plants flat-chased in the panels, on the punched ground common to the three examples. The second cup discussed here *(Fig. 17)* has regular stylized flowers of

39

19

the type seen on New England furniture of the time, and delicately proportioned beaded scroll handles. The third *(Fig. 18)* is more gourd-shaped and stands on a short foot. Here, too, the handles are cast; they have a freedom of design (though not particularly well executed) that characterizes the flat-chased naturalistic motifs and that is typical of the 1680's.

The few pieces that bear Sanderson's mark alone were probably made in the decade after Hull's death. Such is the two-handled cup just mentioned, and such, probably, is the large tankard in the Museum of Fine Arts, Boston *(Fig. 19).* It has the broad drum, narrow baseband, and handle terminal of the early example by Dummer *(see Fig. 4).* However, the thumbpiece is slightly later in style and the flower engraved in the cover is a form of decoration popular in the late 1680's and 1690's *(see Fig. 35).*

No survey of Hull and Sanderson's work

is complete without mention of the porringer and spoon, forms that became commonplace in later periods. The earliest type of porringer has a slightly domed bottom with sides curving out to a straight lip; the handle is a simple, pierced trefoil shape. The earliest spoons are "slip-end," with a slim strip handle tapered at the end into a wedge shape, and a beautifully designed fig-shaped bowl *(see Fig. 27).* By the 1660's the "Puritan" spoon became fashionable *(Fig. 20).* Here the bowl is more rounded and the handle is simply cut off straight at the end. So simple in design but so beautifully proportioned, these early spoons are extremely attractive objects.

Jeremiah Dummer was also an eminent figure in Boston and, like his master John Hull, participated in merchant activities. He became a selectman, member of the Council of Safety, constable, justice of the peace, judge of the Superior Court, treasurer of Suffolk County, and captain of his Artillery Company. In other words, he was one of the leading citizens of Boston, whose natural and inevitable duty it was, in the manner of European landed gentry, to share the executive responsibilities of government. Dummer had merchant interests in Europe and sent one of his sons to a university in Holland, while another of his sons became lieutenant governor of Massachusetts.

Considerably more of Dummer's silver survives than Hull's or Sanderson's, and he worked well into the following style period. His range of forms also includes small cups, mugs, salvers, and standing salts. Some of these will be discussed in the next chapter.

Two-handled cups by Dummer survive in a form identical to the late ones by Hull and Sanderson, and those by Sanderson alone. He utilized handle molds identical to those used on the pieces shown in Figures 17 and 18, and he employed flat-chased decoration similar to that on the Coney two-handled cup *(see Fig. 7)*. Dummer's two-handled cup in the First Church of Christ, New Haven *(Fig. 21)* exemplifies the style of his earliest cups. The body is set on a stepped bottom, and is ample in proportion, while the handles form a subtle counterpoint of reverse curves, being an unusual and pleasing combination of beaded, scroll, and caryatid handles. A cup made for the First Church of Dorchester in 1684 *(Fig. 22)* has a rather fatter body and shorter neck,

with striking scroll handles of a type Hull and Sanderson had used on a cup given to the Dedham, Massachusetts, church. Coney also made exactly this type of cup. Dummer followed his master's pattern in making small dram cups *(see Fig. 2)* although in a plain style. A somewhat later development is his cup with elongated body *(Fig. 23)*. In the ensuing, fully-developed Baroque period, Dummer elongated the body of such cups further and added gadrooning and fluting to the lower part.

Several varieties of beaker by Dummer exist. He made small examples with punched decoration and without a base-

20

---

19. Tankard, *ca.* 1680–90, by Robert Sanderson; H. 8 3/16 inches. Courtesy of Museum of Fine Arts, Boston. Gift of John S. Ames and Mary Ames Frothingham.

20. Spoon, *ca.* 1660–80, by John Hull and Robert Sanderson; L. 6 7/8 inches. Yale University Art Gallery. New Haven, Connecticut. The Mabel Brady Garvan Collection.

21

22

23

24

21. Two-handled cup, *ca.* 1680–90, by Jeremiah Dummer; H. 3 inches. First Church of Christ, New Haven, Connecticut. Photograph courtesy of Yale University Art Gallery, New Haven.

22. Two-handled cup, *ca.* 1684, by Jeremiah Dummer; H. 4¼ inches. On loan to Museum of Fine Arts, Boston.

23. Two-handled cup, *ca.* 1685–1700, by Jeremiah Dummer; H. 1¹¹⁄₁₆ inches. Yale University Art Gallery, New Haven, Connecticut. The Mabel Brady Garvan Collection.

24. Beaker, *ca.* 1697, by Jeremiah Dummer; H. 6³⁄₁₆ inches. Yale University Art Gallery; New Haven, Connecticut. The Mabel Brady Garvan Collection.

---

band *(see Fig. 1)*; he also made this form plain and with a baseband (such as the example in the First Church, Guilford, Connecticut). Larger beakers made by him also survive, both in the very flared style of Figure 8, and also in the magnificent style of Figure 24, presumably from the same decade. (It does not seem possible to define a chronology for beakers: both the almost tubular and the very flared types appear to have been made simultaneously throughout this early period.) With its broad body and considerable height, abruptly flared mouth and simple inscription, the example *(Fig. 24)* made for the First Church in Ipswich, Massachusetts is a masterpiece. It has the hammered-surface appearance of the best seventeenth-century silver.

Made probably in the 1690's, in a period when elaborate Baroque forms were slowly becoming fashionable, the fine tankard by Dummer *(Fig. 25)* is notable for its successful utilization of cut-card ornament at handle juncture and on the cover. The motif seems to have come from Huguenot silversmiths, via England; the shape of this cut-card (which was actually cut in the desired pattern from a thin sheet of silver and applied) is a variant of the fleur-de-lis. It adds a dimension of richness to the object. Further elaboration was sometimes added to such tankards in the form of deep grooves on the upper surface of the handle between the hinge and the "loop"—about two-thirds of the way down—and a cast cherub's mask applied to the terminal *(see Fig. 76)*. The development in the type of baseband from that on the earlier tankard *(see Fig. 4)* to this should be noted.

Mention must also be made of Dum-

43

25

26

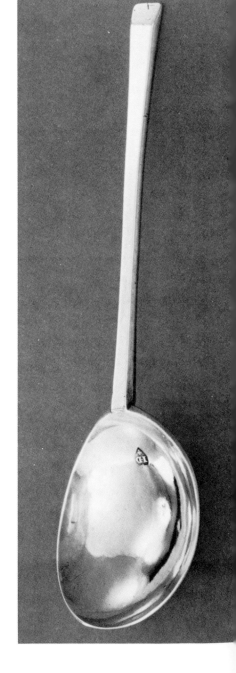

27

44

25. Tankard, *ca.* 1690–1700, by Jeremiah Dummer; H. 5⁷⁄₁₆ inches. Museum of Fine Arts, Boston. Spalding Collection.

26. Porringer, *ca.* 1690–1710, by Jeremiah Dummer; L. 8⅛ inches. Yale University Art Gallery, New Haven, Connecticut. The Mabel Brady Garvan Collection.

27. Spoon, *ca.* 1670–80, by Jeremiah Dummer; L. 7⁵⁄₁₆ inches. Yale University Art Gallery, New Haven, Connecticut. The Mabel Brady Garvan Collection.

28. Spoon, *ca.* 1690–1700, by John Coney; L. 7⅜ inches. Yale University Art Gallery, New Haven, Connecticut. The Mabel Brady Garvan Collection.

29. Two-handled cup, *ca.* 1670–78, by Benjamin Sanderson; H. 2³⁄₁₆ inches. Worcester Art Museum, Worcester, Massachusetts.

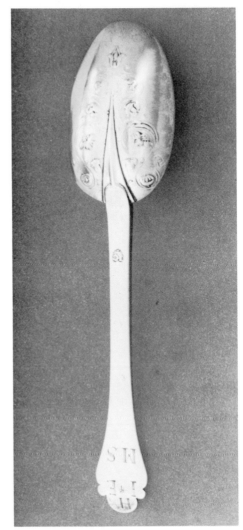

28

mer's great basin (in the First Church, Cambridge, Massachusetts); his porringers *(Fig. 26)*, which show a development from the earlier examples *(see p. 40)* in the form of the handle and the body—now bellied with the lip pinched in; and spoons. Among these is the "slip-end," the earliest type known to have been made in America *(Fig. 27)* and the fine elaborate Baroque type (illustrated here with an example by John Coney *[Fig. 28]*), with beaded, scrolled decoration in relief on the back of the now almost oval bowl, and occasionally on the front of the handle.

John Coney was perhaps the most exceptional of all American silversmiths. His career spanned three different style periods, and monumental examples by him in each style have fortunately survived. Virtually all the silver known to have been made by him is of fine quality, and his best objects are masterpieces of the art. Yet his life illustrates that progressive change in the social status of the silversmith noted in Chapter 1, for he did not play an important role in town government, as Hull or Dummer did. He occupied some minor offices in the colony—Hogreeve, Constable, Tithingman—and

29

30

30. Tankard, *ca.* 1685–95, by John Coney; H. 7⅛ inches. Yale University Art Gallery, New Haven, Connecticut. The Mabel Brady Garvan Collection.

31. Shrimpton arms. Detail of Fig. 30.

32. Spout cup, *ca.* 1690–1710, by John Coney; H. 5 inches. The Heritage Foundation, Old Deerfield, Massachusetts.

engraved paper money for Massachusetts as Dummer had done for Connecticut; otherwise his life appears to have been quiet and discreet.

Coney's career began about 1680; thus, only a few examples of his work in the seventeenth-century styles are known. He made small and large beakers, all of them plain. His contributions to the splendid treasure of the First Church, Ipswich, Massachusetts (now at Yale) were two superb large beakers *(see Fig. 8)*. Early two-handled cups by Coney, (such as those in the First Parish, Concord, Massachusetts) have the broad, low body typical of the 1680's *(see Fig. 22)*. One fine cup in the Congregational Church, Stratford, Connecticut, has handles identical to those used by Dummer *(see Fig. 21)*, and flat-chased ornament in panels, very similar to that used on an attractive small cup by Sanderson's son Benjamin *(Fig. 29)*. His important cup, heavily chased in the Carolean style, has already been discussed *(see Fig. 7)*; only one other example of this form by Coney is known.

Designs similar to those on the two-handled cups, but engraved rather than chased, are found on an early tankard by Coney (in the Winterthur Museum). For tankards he also employed the attractive and early motif of the double-cupped thumbpiece. One of his masterpieces in this form is illustrated in Figure 30. Although this example does not have the long body-drop of the Sanderson tankard *(see Fig. 19)*, all the other seventeenth-century elements are there, including a superbly executed cartouche surrounding the Shrimpton arms *(Fig. 31)*.

At the very end of the century a charming cup design appeared, which eventually developed into the pear-shaped cann of the Queen Anne period. This form was probably based on a ceramic type; Staffordshire slip-ware examples are not uncommon and were popular in America at the time. It is illustrated here utilized as

31

32

33

a spout cup (supposedly for feeding invalids) *(Fig. 32)*, and as an unusual two-handled cup *(Fig. 33)*, by the Boston silversmith Edward Winslow (1669–1753). Winslow's example has seventeenth-century cast handles and a stepped bottom, and is one of his few pieces from this period.

It is a short step from Coney's heavily chased Carolean ornament *(see Fig. 7)* to the lighter drawing of the engraved naturalistic designs that Dummer utilized *(see Fig. 13)*, and which were successfully used on a rare plate by Coney in the Museum of Fine Arts, Boston, and on a salver *(Fig. 34)* by Timothy Dwight (1654–92). That Dwight died at the beginning of the last decade of the century reveals how early this kind of design was popular in Boston. What makes Dwight's piece so unusual is the introduction of a naïve *chinoiserie* into the design. To-

gether with the British royal lion and unicorn are an elephant and a camel symbolizing things Eastern (Chinese and Indian), the passion for which was still unassuaged by the end of the century. Dwight also made a tankard—very English in style but unique for Boston—with chased, repeated acanthus-leaf ornament at the bottom of the body. It also has an unusual lion thumbpiece (eagle thumbpieces were occasionally used, especially by Coney, in this decade). Similarity between the chased ornament on this tankard and that on the Onckelbag cup *(see Fig. 12)* should be noted, while the use of engraved naturalistic designs in New York at this time, in a tighter manner, has also been observed *(see Fig. 10)*.

Another craftsman in Boston at the end of the century who favored this kind of engraved motif *(Fig. 35)* was William Rouse (1639–1705). He also made a very

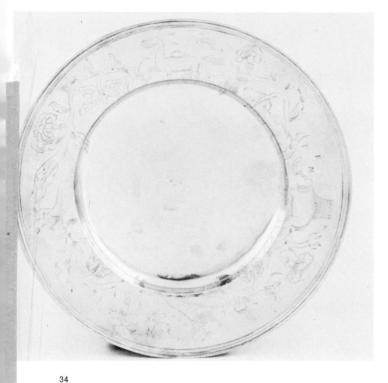

34

35

33. Two-handled cup, *ca.* 1690–1710, by Edward Winslow; H. 4⅝ inches. First Congregational Church, Milford, Connecticut. Photograph courtesy of Yale University Art Gallery, New Haven, Connecticut.

34. Salver, *ca.* 1680–92, by Timothy Dwight; D. 11⅚ inches. Courtesy of Museum of Fine Arts, Boston. Gift of Mr. and Mrs. D. L. Pickman.

35. Patch box, *ca.* 1690–1705, by William Rouse; H. ¹¹⁄₁₆ inches. Yale University Art Gallery, New Haven, Connecticut. The Mabel Brady Garvan Collection.

rare covered skillet *(Fig. 36)* engraved with the Foster arms, directly in the English style. The low cover and the terminal are in the seventeenth-century style, although the scroll bracket feet are seen in a different context in the ensuing period. As a postscript to this survey of seventeenth-century silver in Boston is an illustration of the frequently used feather or crossed-fronds mantling, here shown in a simple version by Edward Winslow *(Fig. 37)*.

New York silversmiths of the seventeenth century occupied the same kind of position in society that Coney appears to have filled in Boston. They were not among the most prominent men of their time, but seem to have been craftsmen first and foremost, content to fill a variety of minor offices in city government.

One of the earliest native silversmiths was Jurian Blanck, Jr. (*ca.* 1645–1714). The son of an immigrant Dutch silversmith, he became a member of the Reformed Dutch Church and in 1672 was appointed to the Office of Weights and Measures. He made several beakers for Reformed Dutch churches in the 1680's similar to the example (which was not made specifically for church use) illustrated here *(Fig. 38)*. We have already

49

36

37

38

seen engraved decoration of this type on beakers by Van der Burch and Hull and Sanderson, and have noted that the stamped foliate band at the base is a specific New York feature. Church beakers frequently contain an engraved reproduction of Faith, Hope, and Charity in pendent ovals, in addition to the birds (or trees, as a variation) above the baseband. An unusual piece of New York church silver of this time is the large and fine baptismal basin by Blanck, made for the Philipse family (and now in the First Reformed Church in Tarrytown).

Blanck made one of the earliest styles of tankard in New York *(Fig. 39)*. With its simple baseband, low cover, and double-cupped thumbpiece, it is very similar to the tankards made in Boston in the 1670's and early 1680's by Jeremiah Dummer *(see Fig. 4)*. Of superior proportions, it is also superbly engraved with the Van Cortlandt arms in a swirling acanthus cartouche. Another masterpiece by Blanck is a two-handled covered cup—the third known in this style (now in the Winterthur Museum). The two others were made by Gerrit Onckelbag in the same city, presumably in the same decade *(see Fig. 12)*.

In New York, spoons were frequently given to pallbearers at funerals and marked with the deceased's name, age, and the date. The early ones are charac-

39

36. Covered skillet, *ca.* 1690–1705, by William Rouse; H. 4⅝ inches. Yale University Art Gallery, New Haven, Connecticut. Lent by Mr. and Mrs. Donald Henry.

37. Palmes arms. Detail of a plate, *ca.* 1680–1700, by Edward Winslow. Courtesy of Museum of Fine Arts, Boston.

38. Beaker, *ca.* 1680–1700, by Jurian Blanck, Jr.; H. 6⅝ inches. Yale University Art Gallery, New Haven, Connecticut. The Mabel Brady Garvan Collection.

39. Tankard, *ca.* 1680–1700, by Jurian Blanck, Jr.; H. 6½ inches. Museum of the City of New York. Gift of Augustus van Cortlandt.

40

41

teristically Dutch, and dissimilar from anything made in New England *(Fig. 40)*. They were made in two parts rather than cast in one (as in New England), while the bowl was round and hammered rather than cast and fig-shaped. Extremely complex by comparison with the simplicity of the early Boston examples, the handles are composed of incised scrolls with a terminal in the form of a caryatid, a hoof, or an owl. These spoons are inferior to New England examples aesthetically, however, for the casting was often of poor quality.

This example is one of three known to have survived.

Cornelius van der Burch died before the turn of the century, thus he did not work into the full Baroque period. He was appointed alderman in 1664, and high constable in 1689, also serving in the Office of Weights and Measures. Among the few pieces now known to have been made by him, the Sandersen beaker *(see Fig. 9)* is one of the masterpieces of its time. The stamped and cast baseband of his fine tankard, with a later corkscrew thumbpiece (in the Museum of the City of New York) is an interesting variation of the baseband seen on the beaker. Van der Burch made funeral spoons, a small tumbler or beaker identical to Dutch and English types and popular in New York at this time, and a splendid small octagonal trencher salt *(Fig. 41)*. This form succeeded the standing salt of medieval origin, which is known in America only in examples of the William and Mary style. The Van der Burch trencher salts are probably the earliest known. Their small size, lovely proportions, and superior workmanship make them admirable objects.

42

40. Spoon, *ca.* 1670–90, by Jurian Blanck, Jr.; L. 6¾ inches. Yale University Art Gallery, New Haven, Connecticut. The Mabel Brady Garvan Collection.

41. Trencher salt, *ca.* 1690–99, by Cornélius van der Burch; H. 1⅜ inches. Museum of the City of New York. Lent by Dr. John Jay DuBois.

42. Two-handled bowl, *ca.* 1690–1710, by Jacob Boelen; H. 2¼ inches. Yale University Art Gallery, New Haven, Connecticut. The Mabel Brady Garvan Collection.

Jacob Boelen (*ca.* 1654–1729) worked well into the subsequent style period, and indeed made one of its masterpieces (*see Fig. 57*). He was fairly active civically—assessor for the North Ward of his city, alderman, brantmaster, special assessor, and appointed to various committees for improving main streets and building the new City Hall. He made two typical beakers for the Utrecht Reformed Church of Brooklyn, and several tankards with corkscrew thumbpieces and bands of stamped foliate ornament at the base. Most of these tankards have coins set into the lid—another typical New York practice. Boelen also made a spout cup, unusual for this city, in a style almost identical to that of Boston (*see Fig. 32*); and variants of the dram cup (*Fig. 42*). This example has a more conventionally bowl-shaped body than the Hull and Sanderson types (*see Fig. 2*), but the same stepped foot, twisted wire handles, and chased panels with naturalistic decoration. Typical of New York is the heavily chased plant of this example compared to the flat-chasing of Boston. Aesthetically, the chasing is too heavy for the body of this little cup; a successful synthesis is not achieved until the bowl has expanded to a larger size (*see Fig. 11*). Boelen did make an example of the larger bowl, with cast caryatid handles and a stamped foliate baseband on the foot. Similar small bowls, both plain and chased, were made by other silversmiths in New York at this time, such as Van der Spiegel and Henricus Boelen.

Bartholomew Le Roux (*ca.* 1663–1713) was one of the earliest immigrant Huguenot silversmiths working in America. By him, his sons, and apprentices some of the finest silver of the next two style periods was made. Perhaps his most interesting seventeenth-century piece is the two-handled bowl illustrated in Figure 43.

43

Somewhat simpler in execution than the elaborate Kierstede example already discussed, but unfortunately slightly disfigured by later engraving, the bowl has a distinctive, low, rounded profile and geometrical chasing. Its lobed form becomes more obvious in the absence of bold chasing; the regular rhythms of its movement prefigure the William and Mary style. Le Roux also made a pair of beautiful trencher salts in the English manner for the De Peyster family, a vivid witness to his skill in their simplicity, quality of execution, and excellent proportions (on loan to the Metropolitan Museum).

Gerrit Onckelbag was the stepson of Ahasuerus Hendricks, one of the earliest New York silversmiths, and was probably

43. Two-handled bowl, *ca.* 1680–1700, by Bartholomew Le Roux; H. 5½ inches. Yale University Art Gallery, New Haven, Connecticut. The Mabel Brady Garvan Collection.

44. Tankard, *ca.* 1695–1710, by Cornelius Kierstede; H. 7¾ inches. Yale University Art Gallery, New Haven, Connecticut. The Mabel Brady Garvan Collection.

45. Tankard by Cornelius Kierstede. Front view of Fig. 44.

trained by him. Onckelbag played no significant part in the city government and, indeed, was later convicted of counterfeiting. His superb two-handled cup has already been discussed (*see Fig. 12*). He made typical New York church beakers

44

45

and also an example of the New York two-handled bowl mentioned above, as well as the thoroughly English type of two-handled cup made also in Boston (*see Fig. 22*). Of imposing size, Onckelbag's example (in the Yale University Art Gallery) is engraved with the Van Cortlandt arms; two other examples of this form by Van der Burch and Blanck have survived. They lack the grace and harmonious proportions of the smaller bowls, however.

Cornelius Kierstede's career began at the end of the seventeenth century, and his chief contribution to the art of American silversmithing lies in the following period. Indeed, it is questionable whether or not the objects discussed in this chapter were actually made in this century. They exemplify the transition from one style to another. One of the finest of all New York tankards, by Kierstede, is illustrated here (*Fig. 44*). Its baseband is enriched with meander-wire (thin wire in a zigzag pattern) and a stamped foliate band, and its cover flange is lavishly engraved. Below the corkscrew thumbpiece is a cast lion applied to the handle, while a cast cherub's mask is applied to the handle terminal. The engraved arms (unidentified) are surrounded by a rich acanthus cartouche with the characteristic New York fruit swags below (*Fig. 45*). In the profusion of its ornament and the rich rhythms of its decoration, it is very much an early Baroque object. Kierstede made several tankards, but only one other (at Colonial Williamsburg) matches the lavishness of this.

CHAPTER THREE

46

Baroque

Silver of the

William and Mary Period

47

For much of the time from the 1690's to the second decade of the eighteenth century, the American colonies found themselves deeply involved in England's crucial struggle to achieve military and political equality with France and Spain. War alternatively depressed and immensely stimulated the economy of the colonies during this period. An increasing awareness of their political and economic importance to England heightened the colonists' self-esteem, while the war quickened their life and widened their horizons. A great expansion in cultural life occurred in these years.

Between 1690 and 1720, Boston's population expanded from seven to twelve

46. Standing cup, *ca.* 1700, by Jeremiah Dummer; H. *ca.* 8 inches. Courtesy of Museum of Fine Arts, Boston.

47. Two-handled covered cup, 1701, by John Coney; H. 10¼ inches. Harvard University, Cambridge, Massachusetts. Gift of the Hon. William Stoughton.

thousand, that of New York from about four to seven thousand, and that of Philadelphia from a size equal to New York to over ten thousand. Consequent upon this growth of population was an increase in the physical size of the towns; much building was completed, new roads laid out, bridges built, docks and wharves improved and ships built, and previously unpopulated areas developed. Richer inhabitants built many fine brick houses for themselves in each of the three cities, while the civic authorities erected handsome city halls and market places of brick. Perhaps the greatest expansion took place in Philadelphia, and also the greatest economic growth; in the years 1699 to 1702, for instance, trade in that port increased to such an extent that customs receipts multiplied almost sixfold.

Economic growth also broadened people's lives and minds. The spread of Anglicanism helped to dispel the rigidness of the Nonconformist Church in Boston and the narrow provincialism of the Dutch in New York. The presence of royal governors, with their attendants and rituals, introduced a new element of luxury in the two cities. Fashionable citizens quickly sought to emulate the manners and attitudes of these "aristocrats."

More fine taverns and coffee houses appeared, coaches became commonplace, fairs, festivities, and musical events grew apace, and the ever proliferating trade brought in from Europe and the Indies a large variety of such luxurious stuffs as "flowered Venetian Silks of the newest Fashion." Periwig-makers, dancing masters, painters, jewelers, watchmakers, and gardeners found sufficient patronage. Schools were founded, newspapers were established, and libraries expanded. Daniel Neal's comment on Boston life, written in 1718, is worth repeating here because it sums up the attitudes and aspirations of all the colonists who admired luxuries and regularly patronized silversmiths:

> A gentleman from London would almost think himself at home in Boston, when he observes the numbers of the people, their houses, their furniture . . . their dress, and conversation, which is perhaps as splendid and showy as that of the most considerable tradesmen in London. . . . In the concerns

of their civil life, as in their dress, tables, and conversation, they affect to be as much English as possible. . . . There is no fashion in London but in three or four months it is to be seen at Boston.

American Baroque silver reflects the considerable enrichment of life in America in this period. We have already seen elaborate ornament in the Carolean manner appearing on Boston and New York silver in the last decade of the seventeenth century—rather heavy but free naturalistic forms at first, later becoming more regular and geometrical in their repetition. In the period generally called "William and Mary," ornament was mainly of a stylized geometrical type, particularly with marked rhythm in depth, such as fluting and its reverse, gadrooning. Baroque vigor was expressed fully in three dimensions, with tense and vivid rhythms moving in and out of the mass of the object as well as on the vertical and horizontal axes.

Although American silver has frequently been described as "plain" and "direct," this period abounds in objects that are as complex and elaborate as most of their European counterparts. Yet, with all but the finest objects of this time there is an ever-present feeling that elegance, ornament, and sophistication are overlaid on a basically intransigent material. Comparison with the often over-elaborate crestrails of William and Mary chairs might be invoked. Only with the masterpieces of the period is it apparent that the silversmith achieved a full synthesis of form and ornament. With these, one comes to feel that the material was almost fluid in the handling, and that it willingly and gracefully assumed the elaborate shapes the silversmith devised.

The finest silversmiths of this period were Coney, Dummer, and Winslow in Boston; Boelen, Kierstede, Van der Spiegel, Bartholomew Le Roux, and his probable apprentice Peter van Dyck (1684–1751) in New York. Only the latter made no important silver in the seventeenth-century styles; and only he and Coney made masterpieces in the Queen Anne style. Indicative of the new sophistication of this period and an increased demand for luxuries is the appearance of new forms, such as chocolate pots, teapots, punch bowls, and boxes and shakers for sugar, all very elaborately wrought.

The earliest precisely datable pieces of silver in the William and Mary style were made in 1700–1701, although it must be repeated that Baroque forms had appeared during the preceding decade. Of these pieces, a standing cup by Jeremiah Dummer given to the church in Eastham, Massachusetts, is dated 1700 *(Fig. 46)*. In basic form it recalls late Hull and Sanderson cups, and Dummer himself made a plain version of it in seventeenth-century style. Typical of this period is the overlaying of new ornament on an older form —a highly successful combination here. The band of alternate gadrooning and fluting on the lower half of the cup serves to accentuate the outward thrust of the body from the narrow stem; it is also swirled, which doubly emphasizes this and tends to lead the eye around the mass of the cup. The lip gently repeats the outward movement of this band of ornament, while the band on the foot echoes it on a smaller scale. The stem also has a rhythm of inward and outward movement. Another example of this type of cup, superior in execution, was purchased by the First Church, Dorchester, Massachusetts, from the bequest of Sir William Stoughton, the lieutenant governor of the Colony, whose will was proved in 1701; the cup is so dated. This example is engraved with a richly swirling cartouche surrounding the Stoughton arms.

Also associated with Stoughton is the monumental two-handled covered cup by John Coney *(Fig. 47)*, given by the lieutenant governor to Harvard College in 1701. Details of the presentation can be found in the fascinating diary of Samuel Sewall, wherein the cup is variously described as a "grace cup," "cup," and "bowl." Its connection with the seventeenth century is obvious: We have seen the cast handles before, although they are here given extra flourishes at the scrolled terminal. And the broad, plain expanse of the body of the piece recalls Coney's own massive two-handled cup in an earlier style *(see Fig. 6)*. Yet the differences are equally obvious. The cup is set on a higher foot that is splayed, so that the eye is led in from its edge to the bottom of the body, and enriched with a band of fluted ornament between two plain bands. Thus, a rhythm of ornamented and plain bands, of projection and recession vertically (recalling the rhythms of William and Mary chair stiles), horizontally, and in depth, is established. The body bursts out and up, as in the Dummer cup—a movement emphasized by the band of gadrooned and fluted ornament that leads to, and contrasts with, the plain central area of the body. The subtly domed cover repeats the alternating rhythms of elaborate and plain bands of the foot, utilizing the same kind of ornament and leading, again in depth, to the apex, which is crowned by the lobed ball finial. As a final enrichment, Coney engraved the donor's arms in a superb cartouche of swirling acanthus leaves, so much richer and more vivid than the cartouche on his earlier cup *(see Fig. 6)*, and closely comparable to New York cartouches of the time *(see Figs. 10 and 12)*.

Only one other cup of this magnitude has survived from this time, and it may date from the end of the period. It is a slightly larger example by Edward Winslow, which descended in the Lowell family of Boston *(Fig. 48)*. The foot is of similar form but is higher, giving a feeling of elevation to the piece that we shall see more fully expressed in the following period. Not only is the foot higher

48

49

---

48. Two-handled covered cup, *ca.* 1705–15, by Edward Winslow; H. 10⅞ inches. Yale University Art Gallery, New Haven, Connecticut. The Mabel Brady Garvan Collection.

49. Sugar box, *ca.* 1700–1710, by John Coney; H. 4¹³⁄₁₆ inches. Courtesy of Museum of Fine Arts, Boston. Bequest of Charles Hitchcock Tyler.

but the band of emphatic gadrooning (not alternated with fluting here) is wider and gives more of an upward thrust. The plain area above this band is more nearly equal in width to the gadrooning, making for a more consistent and regular rhythm than on the Coney cup. At the lip is another band of gadrooning. The cover is also domed, with a lobed ball finial, but with only one band of gadrooning. There is an obvious difference in the handles; Winslow employed the unadorned hollow type (not unknown to seventeenth-century silversmiths, who had used it on tankards) rather than the intricate cast kind. These unite two bands of gadrooning and contribute, in their simplicity and elegance, an effect of smoother rhythms and transitions.

Despite their slightly different heights it is instructive to note that both these cups measure ten units high to eleven wide; in other words, they are almost square. Yet they give the marked impression of being higher than the seventeenth-century two-handled covered cup by Coney (see Fig. 6). The Winslow cup (forty ounces) weighs a third again as much as the early Coney cup.

Coney's sugar boxes are also enriched with the boldly marked rhythmic decoration characteristic of the 1690's. His finest example, a superb, tightly controlled Baroque object, is illustrated here (Fig. 49). A shallow oval covered box (not only a container for sugar but presumably for other precious items, such as spices or jewels), it stands on four scrolled bracket feet. Thus, it is supported above the ground and has space on all sides, in the manner of highboys of the period compared to earlier chests. This emphasizes the mass and highlights the effect of projection and recession. Around the body are chased twelve massive oval lobes reminiscent of the lip of Dummer's two-handled cup (see Fig. 13), although heavier and fuller here. To accentuate

these convex lobes, deep flutes are chased between them, while above is a plain area. Although the flange of the cover is plain, the lobes are repeated above, on a smaller scale and with a more insistent rhythm. Above the band of lobes is a punched ground on which acanthus leaves are chased, directly recalling Onckelbag's New York cups (see Fig. 12). The handle of the cover is in the form of a coiled snake within a heavily chased oval.

Within the fairly small confines of this box (it is only eight and three-eighths inches long) is set up an enormous amount of rhythm and movement. Yet it is all controlled—by a subtle use of mass, by contrasting plain and elaborate areas, and by a series of repetitions on the oval form.

As Winslow and Coney were the only Boston silversmiths whose two-handled covered cups survive from this period, so they were also responsible for almost all of the surviving boxes. Winslow made one of these for his personal use, and it descended in his family (Fig. 50). It is even more elaborately wrought than Coney's; its wealth of ornamented design fully expresses its function as a treasure chest. Again oval and also standing on four scrolled bracket feet (but not the corkscrew variety Coney employed, which are reminiscent of tankard thumbpieces), the body is decorated with a gadrooned band at the bottom, then groups of alternate gadrooning and fluting swirled around medallions at front, back, and each side, thus accentuating the oval form. Rich acanthus-leaf detail on a punched ground rises above each leg and between the groups of gadrooning. Above the whole is a plain band below the cover. While the front medallion is covered by a cartouche-shaped hasp, with a chased shield within an acanthus surround, the side and rear medallions are chased with small chivalric scenes—the box may well have been a wedding gift. (Many of the motifs used here can be found on Italian Renaissance

50

50. Sugar box, *ca.* 1700–1710, by Edward
Winslow; H. 5⅜ inches. Yale University Art
Gallery, New Haven, Connecticut. The Mabel
Brady Garvan Collection.

51

51. Monteith bowl, *ca.* 1700–1710, by John Coney; H. 8⅝ inches. Yale University Art Gallery, New Haven, Connecticut. The Mabel Brady Garvan Collection.

52. Colman arms. Detail of Fig. 51.

clearly in this illustration; indeed, it is so intricately wrought that several small holes appear, not from long use but from the silversmith's having pushed the material to its very limits in the search for the fullest expressiveness. Complex acanthus foliage spills over the cover, and cherubs or angels fly within a heavy oval frame. The handle is a variation of the acanthus motif.

In their intricate patterns these boxes convey the same effects that cabinetmakers sought in their use of rich burl veneering and japanning, both popular in this period. Furthermore, picture frames of this time, enclosing portraits of men and women with highly intricate, curled wigs, were often oval and frequently utilized swirled groups of gadrooning and fluting. While the Coney box is bold and vigorous, the Winslow piece is one of the choicest of American Baroque objects in its subtle use of point and counterpoint, smooth and elaborate, naturalistic and geometric forms, its infinite variations on the scroll and the oval, its capricious highlights, its intricate rhythms.

Standing at the apex of all American silver is the monumental Monteith bowl by John Coney *(Fig. 51)*. Massive, highly sophisticated, unique in its period, this bowl surely symbolizes the aspirations and compass of American taste of the time. The use of so ostentatious an object for so modest a purpose—to hold iced water in which to cool wine glasses, suspending them upside down with the foot over the rim—reveals a self-conscious elegance. The form originated in England; this particular piece is no less ornate than contemporary English examples.

Although design elements appear that we have seen before—such as the splayed, gadrooned foot—Coney's use of the subtle, fluid fluting to complement rather than accentuate the bold upward curve of the body was inspired. It gives a shimmering rather than an insistent rhythmical high-

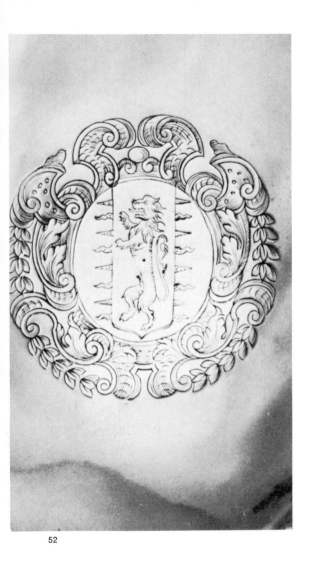

52

wedding chests.) On the cover there is an obvious rhythm of plain and worked bands, meander-wire at the edge of the flange, and a small band of bold gadrooning. The top of the cover is so elaborately chased that it is difficult to understand

light and leads the eye immediately to the complex rim area, the focal point of the bowl. On a punched, matted ground, and with an architectural, intricately scrolled outline above, Baroque corbels are applied beneath a series of cherub's-head finials, with flowers and chased acanthus foliage swirling round. At each side is applied a massive lion's-head mask with mouth open and holding the hinge for the Baroque-form, swivel handle. Inside are engraved the Colman arms within the Baroque-style cartouche that appeared late in this period *(Fig. 52)*. All the style elements of the period are here; yet the rhythms are unusually varied and the rim area is an obvious tour de force. Its successful integration of chased, cast, and engraved ornaments, its great size, and its harmonious proportions make the Monteith indubitably one of the greatest of all pieces of American silver.

Equally luxurious, although smaller in scale, is the chocolate pot by Edward Winslow *(Fig. 53)*. It is a rich object, designed for what must have seemed to its owners an exotic purpose. Obviously derived from English prototypes, it is unlike any form we have yet seen in American silver. The tall body is curved at the bottom and set on a low splayed foot, and it tapers toward the very high dome of the cover. Bands of gadrooned ornament of varying width alternate with plain areas, which are also articulated by fine molded strips serving as rhythmic variations. On top of the cover around the broad high finial (which is removable to permit the insertion of a rod to keep the chocolate stirred), there is an area of cut-card ornament as a further variation. Thumbpiece and chain around the finial are extra flourishes. The handle, it should be noticed, is at right angles to the spout (generally a convention with chocolate pots, and presumably to allow the liquid to be stirred from the top while pouring). The spout has a swan-neck shape with acanthus embellishments at bottom and top;

aesthetically, it is a strange appendage to what is otherwise a well-ordered geometrical form, and it seems to echo much earlier shapes. Form and decoration, however, have been closely unified by the silversmith, with excellent variations in rhythmic movement and a tight control.

Another extremely rare object from the beginning of the William and Mary period is a standing salt *(Fig. 54)* by the partnership of John Allen and John Edwards (*ca.* 1695–*ca.* 1710). Its form can be traced back to the medieval "great salts"; it was highly regarded in the seventeenth century, meriting separate mention in the inventories of wealthy households. Three American standing salts have survived (the others are by Dummer and Winslow), and all were made in this period. All are octagonal, with one or two bands of gadrooning. Since top and bottom are so similar in design and seem to join at the central point of the molding on the stem, the repetition of gadrooning at top and bottom would seem to be a necessary balance in the design. The Allen and Edwards piece is probably the most successful, for the gadrooning is also swirled—an attractive touch, adding an element of the curvilinear to a geometrical design composed mainly of straight lines. The top of the piece is concave to hold the salt (a luxury at the time), while the four scrolled brackets were intended to support a plate or draped napkin. The boldness of the object, with its strong facets and highlights, indicates the ceremonial importance of its function.

The final New England object in this selection is not so rare as those previously discussed. But it is a lovely form and typifies the silver of this period *(Fig. 55)*. It

53. Chocolate pot, *ca.* 1700–1715, by Edward Winslow; H. 9½ inches. The Metropolitan Museum of Art, New York. Bequest of A. T. Clearwater, 1933.

53

54. Standing salt, *ca.* 1700–1710, by John Allen and John Edwards; H. 5¾ inches. Yale University Art Gallery, New Haven, Connecticut. Lent by Sarah Hayward Draper.

55. Two-handled cup, *ca.* 1705–15, by William Cowell; H. 4³⁄₁₆ inches. Yale University Art Gallery, New Haven, Connecticut. The Mabel Brady Garvan Collection.

was made by William Cowell (1682–1736), who had probably been an apprentice of Dummer; indeed, Dummer had added Baroque ornament to his earlier type of two-handled cup (*see Fig. 23*) to achieve something in the manner of a prototype for this example. Cowell devised elegant proportions for his cup. Where the beading on the handles repeats in miniature the gadrooning on the body, we see the constant interplay of surfaces and reflections typical of the silver of this period. It is interesting to note that Cowell made cups of this type at least as late as 1721 (in the First Church, Dorchester, Massachusetts).

New York silversmiths of this period contrived to make masterpieces of the art, bold, vigorous, and handsome. Of these makers, Cornelius Kierstede was one of the finest. His bowl and tankards have already been discussed—objects that are actually Baroque in their ornateness. Perhaps the greatest of all his silver is the pair of candlesticks and the accompanying snuffer stand in the Metropolitan Museum (*Fig. 56*). Monumental in size and form, they give an indelible impression of the richness of cultured life in New York in this time. They bring to mind the comment of one of the first English governors of New York to Charles II: "I find these people have the breeding of courts, and I cannot conceive how such is acquired."

Kierstede obviously strove for richness of effect, and achieved his aim. Bands of alternate gadrooning and fluting on the candlesticks—swirled on the foot but vertical on the flanges—are bold but not overlarge. The wide bands of molding with applied meander-wire at the top and bottom of the shaft give superb horizontal and

55

56

57

56. Pair of candlesticks and snuffer stand, *ca.* 1700–15, by Cornelius Kierstede; H. (candlesticks) 11½ inches. The Metropolitan Museum of Art, New York. Gift of Robert L. Cammann, 1957, and gift of Mrs. Clermont L. Barnwell, 1964, and Mr. and Mrs. William A. Moore, 1923.

57. Teapot, *ca.* 1705–15, by Jacob Boelen; H. 6½ inches. The Metropolitan Museum of Art, New York. Gift of Mrs. Lloyd K. Garrison, 1961.

vertical rhythm to the column, which, as an extra enrichment, is stop-fluted (the flutes being filled with gadroons for part of their length). The plain facets of the column link the rich areas perfectly. Acanthus leaves spill over each corner, expanding as they descend. The plain area at the bottom of the foot consummately balances the engraved, splayed area below the lower flange. Here is another version of American *chinoiserie,* with exotic people and birds nicely engraved on each face. The accompanying snuffer stand is a bizarre object, in which richness of detail competes with a disunified form not notable for its beauty. Yet it must be admitted that as an example of Baroque extravagance this object also achieves its purpose.

Winslow's chocolate pot was a new form in America, designed for a fashionably new luxury, and the teapot by Jacob Boelen of New York was a similar novelty *(Fig. 57).* It is one of the earliest known in the colonies, although the lieutenant governor of Massachusetts, Sir William Stoughton, owned one before 1701 (as recorded in his inventory). A rich, vivid object, it is fully unified, with exuberant rhythms flowing mainly from the engraved cartouche. The repetition of meander-wire at base and lip, and the change from stamped geometrical ornament at the base to gadrooning on the cover are imaginative touches. Naturalistic forms are also chased on the cover. Here the straight spout, notable for its length and taper, is completely absorbed into the total design.

As monumental in appearance as the Allen and Edwards standing salt is the bold sugar caster by Bartholomew Le Roux *(Fig. 58).* The wide flange of the base provides a strong support for the tall column. Decoration consists as much of molding and piercing as gadrooning, and is expertly used. The broad perforated area of the cover serves as an effective surface for scrolled decoration, leading up to the richer effect of the same naturalistic forms

chased on the top around the knopped finial. It is the most superb of all American casters in size, proportion, and execution.

Salvers, derived from the ancient paten (whose similar purpose was to avoid spillage of liquids), appeared in this period in New York and Boston. They are distinguished from later examples by a band of gadrooning at the edge of the tray and foot; when the gadrooning is swirled, an extra dimension of movement is added. The boldest were made in New York *(Fig. 59).* The example here by Jacobus van der Spiegel is enriched with swirled alternate gadrooning and fluting of such a size as to give a very powerful sense of movement in all dimensions, as well as strong highlights.

Peter van Dyck's rich tankard for the Wendell family *(Fig. 60)* is a marvelous Baroque object, and, apparently, unique. He incorporated the meander-wire and stamped foliate ornament we have noted on seventeenth-century pieces from this city, in addition to gadrooning and engraving on the cover. Chased leaves on a boss in the center of the cover also appear on the Le Roux caster and the Boelen teapot. Contributing to the richness of this object is the fully Baroque appliqué of mask and swags of fruit spilling down the handle. The final embellishment is a superb swirling cartouche engraved on the front of the body, so large and bold that it occupies most of the area of the drum *(Fig. 61).* While Boston silversmiths made several examples of tankards with gadrooning on the cover, this is the only known New York piece.

John Coney's brilliance as a craftsman is fully attested by the silver he made

---

58. Caster, *ca.* 1700–1710, by Bartholomew Le Roux; H. 8 inches. Yale University Art Gallery, New Haven, Connecticut. The Mabel Brady Garvan Collection.

58

59

in each of the three style periods in which he worked, but in none more than this. He maintained a high level of quality throughout the range of his wares. Not all are as ambitious or elaborate as those already discussed in this chapter, however. One of his earliest objects in the Baroque style appears relatively plain by comparison—a small chocolate pot given by Sir William Stoughton to his niece and dated 1701 *(Fig. 62)*. We have already seen a rather similar cover, finial, and beaded ornament in Coney's work *(see Fig. 32)*, and have noted the use of cut-card decoration from the 1690's onward. The double molding on the collar below the finial of Coney's chocolate pot appears also on the Winslow pot *(see Fig. 53)*, and this type of baseband on tankards of the William and Mary period. Combined with the beading and the cut-card appliqué, the elaborate molding used here gives a richness to this choice object that the plain surfaces otherwise belie. Of a shape infrequently used in this country (John Edwards made a smaller

59. Salver, *ca.* 1700–1708, by Jacobus van der Spiegel; D. 8¼ inches. Courtesy of The Henry Francis du Pont Winterthur Museum, Winterthur, Delaware.
60. Tankard, *ca.* 1705–15, by Peter van Dyck; H. 7⅜ inches. Yale University Art Gallery, New Haven, Connecticut. The Mabel Brady Garvan Collection.
61. Wendell arms. Detail of Fig. 60.

example with cut-card ornament on the cover [now in the Worcester Art Museum]), this pot conveys the impression of unassuming richness and strength.

Boston makers utilized gadrooning on tankard covers in this period, as did Peter van Dyck in New York *(see Fig. 60)*. Coney, Dummer, and Winslow all made examples of this form. The example by Coney illustrated here *(Fig. 63)* shows how attractive the feature could be. Combined with a dolphin-and-mask thumbpiece and a cast cherub's-mask on the terminal, it enriches the handsome form at

60

61

which Coney excelled. Other Boston makers of this time occasionally added deep grooves to the tankard handle *(see Fig. 76)*, while Henry Hurst, of Swedish extraction *(ca.* 1665–1717), added the typical New York motif of flower and fruit swags *(Fig. 64)*. In addition to this, Hurst engraved the cover with a band of naturalistic forms in the manner of his native country. Coney occasionally added a small finial to the flat cover of tankards.

Coney's use of gadrooned ornament extended to a unique candlestick with baluster stem *(Fig. 65)*, and to a unique small tripod bowl *(Fig. 66)*, whose function re-

62. Chocolate pot, *ca.* 1700–1710, by John Coney; H. 7⅞ inches. Courtesy of Museum of Fine Arts, Boston.

63. Tankard, *ca.* 1700–1710, by John Coney; H. 7⅝ inches. Worcester Art Museum, Worcester, Massachusetts. Gift of Albert W. Rice.

---

mains obscure. Along with the other Boston makers of the time, he made handsome salvers with gadrooned edges *(see Fig. 73)* and trencher salts with gadrooned tops *(see Fig. 77)*. Both forms occurred in New York at this time also, but were given the

62

63

effect of greater enrichment by their bolder ornament. Fully characteristic of this period is a pair of delightful small cups by Coney, with three bands of different, varying-sized ornamentation and beaded scroll handles *(Fig. 67)*. Obviously related to the spout cup in form *(see Fig. 32)*, they are choice in design and exquisite in scale. Probably dating from the end of this period is a pair of chafing dishes of early type *(Fig. 68)*. These objects were designed to hold heated charcoal in the lower part and to support a plate or vessel on the upper bracket extension of the legs. They were perforated to provide a draft for the charcoal, which gave the craftsman an opportunity to pierce the sides with decorative scrolled or naturalistic designs. Among the earliest examples of this form, they have straighter sides than later dishes and slightly ungainly bracket supports. Coney's work in this period also includes pepper boxes, porringers, spoons, and tobacco boxes, which we shall see later in connection with other makers.

Dummer's chief contributions to the art of silversmithing in the Baroque period are

64. Tankard, *ca.* 1700–1710, by Henry Hurst; H. 6 inches. Courtesy of Museum of Fine Arts, Boston. Gift of Mr. and Mrs. D. L. Pickman.

65. Candlestick, *ca.* 1700–1710, by John Coney; H. 6¾₁₆ inches. Courtesy of Museum of Fine Arts, Boston. Gift of Mr. and Mrs. D. L. Pickman.

66. Tripod bowl, *ca.* 1700–1710, by John Coney; H. 2½ inches. Yale University Art Gallery, New Haven, Connecticut. The John Marshall Phillips Collection.

67. Pair of cups, *ca.* 1700–15, by John Coney; H. 3⅜ inches. Courtesy of Museum of Fine Arts, Boston. Gift of M. and M. Karolik.

64

65

66

67

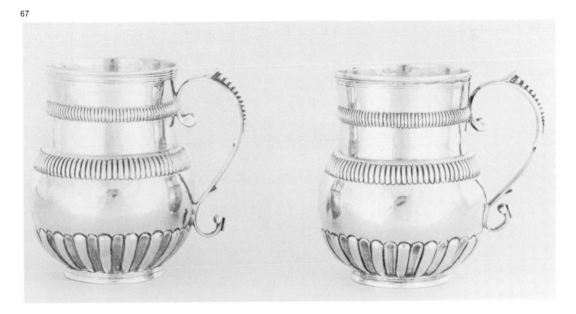

79

his gadrooned and fluted standing cups, of which at least twelve survive, and a standing salt identical to Allen and Edwards's *(see Fig. 54)*, except that the gadrooning is vertical rather than swirled. Dummer also made a very elaborate type of tankard with cut-card ornament on body and cover, deeply grooved handle with a cherub's mask on the terminal, and bold, swirled gadrooning on the cover. One of his choicest forms was a small bell-shaped beaker standing on a low footring (a shape introduced in this period and popular throughout the century) with a broad, swirled, gadrooned and fluted band at the bottom of the body, and a small gadrooned band below the lip. An example illustrated here *(Fig. 69)* also has a small conforming area of punched decoration, in the seventeenth-century style, above the lower ornamented band. Very similar in form to this, though smaller (indeed, almost identical to the cup section of standing cups), is a type of cup with either vertical or swirled ga-

drooning and two cast scroll handles. Coney also made examples of this form.

Edward Winslow's career follows the pattern of Dummer's, without the latter's merchant interests. He occupied many civic offices in his long life: constable in 1699, tithingman in 1703, surveyor in 1705, overseer of the poor in 1711–12 (when he also served on a committee to "prevent and suppress the growth of disorders" in Boston), and selectman in 1714. His death notice in the *Boston Evening Post* for December 3, 1753, gives an excellent illustration of his qualities and position in life:

. . . about 9 o'clock, after a long Indisposition, died Edward Winslow, Esq., who had just entered the 85th year of his Age. This Gentleman had formerly, for many Years, been High Sheriff of the County of Suffolk, and Colonel of the Regiment of Militia in this Town; but by Reason of Age and Infirmities of Body, laid down those Posts, and has for several Years past, till his Death, been a Justice of the Peace and

68

of the Quorum, and one of the Justices of the Inferior Court of Common Pleas for the County of Suffolk, and also Treasurer of the said County.

By the time of his death in the middle of the eighteenth century he must have seemed a relic of a different world—a member of the administrative class, a great craftsman with a dominant place in society rather than a comparatively modest artificer.

Winslow's chief works in the Baroque style are the two-handled cup, the chocolate pots, and the sugar boxes previously discussed. He also made gadrooned tankards and salvers, a standing salt, and cups identical to the pair by Coney shown here *(see Fig. 67)*. His fine candlestick *(Fig. 70)* and trefoil salver *(Fig. 71)* are included here, although they represent a transition between the styles of this and the following period. Coney also made a pair of candlesticks of this type, dated 1716. Their multifaceted socket and base definitely evoke the rhythms of fully developed Baroque silver; yet this kind of stem is also seen in the Queen Anne period. The lovely little trefoil salver is a rare and appealing object. Its ornament lies not on the surface but rather in its vivid shape. It probably dates from this transition period, too. Several silversmiths' marks appear in the Baroque period with the same kind of trefoil used as a reserve for initials, particularly in New York. Winslow also made a fine, large basin and a set of plates for the Second Church, Boston, in this period,

69

---

68. Chafing dish, *ca.* 1710–15, by John Coney; H. 3¹⁄₁₆ inches. Courtesy of Museum of Fine Arts, Boston. Gift of Mr. and Mrs. D. L. Pickman.

69. Beaker, *ca.* 1700–1715, by Jeremiah Dummer; H. 5¾ inches. North Congregational Church, Portsmouth, New Hampshire. Photograph courtesy of Yale University Art Gallery, New Haven, Connecticut.

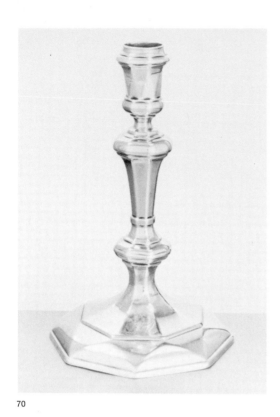

70

71

70. Candlestick, *ca.* 1705–15, by Edward Winslow; H. 7$\frac{1}{16}$ inches. The Colonial Williamsburg Foundation, Williamsburg, Virginia.

71. Salver, *ca.* 1705–15, by Edward Winslow; W. 7$\frac{1}{4}$ inches. Courtesy of The Art Institute of Chicago. Gift of The Antiquarian Society.

72. Serving spoon, *ca.* 1705–15, by Edward Winslow; L. 16$\frac{1}{4}$ inches. Yale University Art Gallery, New Haven, Connecticut. The Mabel Brady Garvan Collection.

---

and one of a splendid set of early flagons for the Brattle Street Church in Boston. The latter is dated 1713 and is very close in style to the example by Peter Oliver shown here *(see Fig. 75)*. Winslow's large serving spoon *(Fig. 72)* with hollow handle, finial, and deep bowl is particularly handsome.

John Edwards (1671–1746) of Boston made a number of excellent objects in this period. He began his career in partnership with John Allen around the turn of the

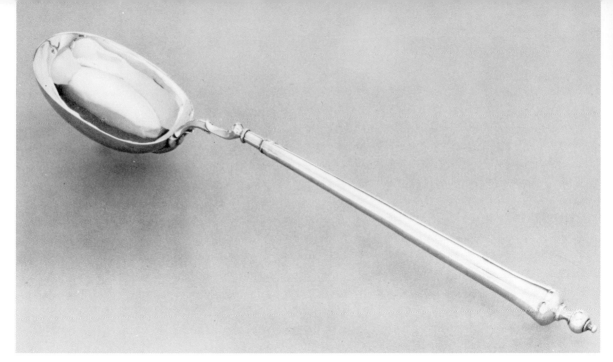

72

century; their most inspired creation is the superb standing salt at Yale *(see Fig. 54)*. Edwards's pieces include a standing cup very similar to the gadrooned and fluted Dummer example *(see Fig. 46)*, as well as plain versions of the form; gadrooned salvers *(Fig. 73)*; plain beakers, both small and large; and an unusual but very attractive two-handled cup with a wide band of gadrooning on the lower part of the body *(Fig. 74)*. This is an ingenious variation of the beaker form and was made for the First Congregational Church, Hatfield, Massachusetts. He also made one of the previously mentioned flagons for the Brattle Street Church, dated 1712.

Among other makers in Boston at this time may be mentioned Peter Oliver (1682–1712), who created an outstanding flagon for the Second Church, Boston, dated 1711 *(Fig. 75)*. It is English in form and seventeenth-century in style, with its broad splayed baseband, double-cupped thumbpiece, and flat cover. Oliver also made a rather squat and sturdy variant of the Winslow chocolate pot. David Jesse (1670–1705), Edward Webb (1666–1718),

Thomas Savage (1664–1749), and Richard Conyers (*ca.* 1668–1708) also made fine silver in this period, while John Noyes (1674–1749) made several excellent tankards and a pair of rather graceless candlesticks, heavily gadrooned and with stop-fluted columns (in the Museum of Fine Arts, Boston).

Although Newport silver is not dealt with at any length in this book, several objects by craftsmen of that city are of importance and interest. The first is a tankard *(Fig. 76)* by Samuel Vernon (1683–1737), which exhibits the William and Mary features we have noted in Boston and New York silver: the stamped leaf ornament on the baseband common in New York, and the handle and thumbpiece frequently used in Boston. The terminal is a variation of the kind common to both cities. Newport's geographical location between the two cities and the constant coastal traffic of the time are ready explanations for this phenomenon. New York characteristics can also be seen in a few pieces of Philadelphia silver that survive from this time.

83

73

74

73. Salver, *ca.* 1700–15, by John Edwards; H. 2½ inches. Yale University Art Gallery, New Haven, Connecticut. The Mabel Brady Garvan Collection.

74. Two-handled cup, *ca.* 1713, by John Edwards; H. 5¾ inches. Yale University Art Gallery, New Haven, Connecticut. The Mabel Brady Garvan Collection.

75. Flagon, 1711, by Peter Oliver; H. 12 inches. Courtesy of The Henry Francis du Pont Winterthur Museum, Winterthur, Delaware.

76. Tankard, *ca.* 1705–15, by Samuel Vernon; H. 7⁵⁄₁₆ inches. Worcester Art Museum, Worcester, Massachusetts. Bequest of Stephen Salisbury III.

77. Trencher salt, *ca.* 1730, by Jacob Ten Eyck; H. 2¼ inches. The Metropolitan Museum of Art, New York. Given in memory of William Bayard van Rensselaer, 1937, by Mrs. van Rensselaer.

75

76

77

Silversmiths in New York carried late-seventeenth-century styles into the first two decades of the eighteenth century. The fairly clear division that occurred in Boston silver of these decades does not appear in New York. Nor, compared to Boston, has anything like the quantity of New York silver survived. Although there are masterpieces, as we have seen—marvelous objects, rich and masculine—the range of secondary pieces from New York is considerably restricted. Beakers, bowls, porringers, spoons, and tankards are the most common forms, while casters, salvers, salts, and sucket forks also appear (the latter are thin, flat strips with a spoon bowl at one end and a two-tined fork at the other and are usually of minimal aesthetic interest).

Jacob Boelen's teapot and his small two-handled bowls from the previous period have already been mentioned. He also made beakers for the New Utrecht Reformed Church of Brooklyn in the typical seventeenth-century Dutch style, one of which is dated 1707. A small spout cup, similar in form to the example by Coney illustrated earlier (see Fig. 32), although quite plain, is also known—a rare early survivor from this city. Some of Boelen's tankards exhibit the New York practice of inserting a foreign coin in the cover, or using one as the handle terminal.

Jacobus van der Spiegel lived only halfway through this period. He made splendid tankards with slightly higher domed covers than the one illustrated earlier (see Fig. 10); his later tankards generally lack the meander-wire ornament, although retaining the stamped leaf band. One fine piece by Van der Spiegel (in the Museum of the City of New York) also bears the marks of Jan van Nieu Kirke. Porringers made in early New York, too, often carry the impression of a different maker's marks, prompting the supposition that some makers cast their handles from molds derived from other makers' objects. A highly unusual and precious object by Van der Spiegel is a gold tablespoon (now at Yale) with a trifid end that is pierced and has three gold bells attached. This maker also created a pair of intricately gadrooned trencher salts, similar to a very fine example shown here (Fig. 77) by Jacob Ten Eyck of Albany (1705–93), who cannot have begun his silversmithing activities much before 1730.

Very few objects by Bartholomew Le Roux are known. Another, smaller version of his caster (see Fig. 58), several small salvers, a chalice for the Episcopal Church of Trenton, New Jersey, and a set of sucket forks constitute virtually his entire known output not already discussed.

Cornelius Kierstede's career is distinguished by various splendid tankards, occasionally with the marks of other New York silversmiths, and occasionally with a coin set in the cover. Superb examples are in the Museum of the City of New York, the Winterthur Museum, and at Colonial Williamsburg. This handsome form was also made in New York in this period by such skilled silversmiths as Bartholomew Schaats (1670–1758) and Benjamin Wynkoop (1675–1728). Kierstede's rare teakettle is difficult to date precisely (Fig. 78). It should be noted that the shape of the body is very close to that of New England two-handled cups of the 1680's (see Fig. 22), while the cover is domed (placing it in the first decade of the eighteenth century at the earliest), and the elaborate spout is of the kind that appeared in the second decade of the century (a less elab-

---

78. Teakettle, ca. 1700–1715, by Cornelius Kierstede; H. 10¼ inches. The Metropolitan Museum of Art, New York. Bequest of James Stevenson van Cortlandt, 1917.

79. Caster, ca. 1700–1715, by Gerrit Onckelbag; H. 3⅜ inches. Collection of Mrs. Edsel B. Ford, Grosse Pointe Shores, Michigan.

78

79

80

81

orate version appears in Figure 87). Kierstede continued to utilize the stamped leaf baseband ornament and to make the type of New York bowl with boldly chased flowers well into the following period, after his removal to Connecticut.

A splendid small caster by Onckelbag is one of the finer New York pieces of this period *(Fig. 79)*. Its cylindrical cover with almost flat top makes it slightly earlier in style than the superb Le Roux example *(see Fig. 58)*. The richness of the high splayed foot, with swirled gadrooning and fluting (a motif echoed on the cover), the stamped leaf ornament above, and the rich moldings distinguish this choice object. The spareness of the pierced ornament on the cover forms a perfect contrast to the rich chasing. Coney also made this early type of caster in Boston in this period, although his is small and lackluster compared to the bold qualities of the Onckelbag example.

Peter van Dyck made a caster in this period of a similar height to Le Roux's and almost as grand (now at Yale). It is beautifully engraved with the Schuyler arms. His mustard pot with gadrooned foot *(Fig. 80)* appears to be unique; it is closely patterned after Dutch examples. He also made a rare covered porringer *(Fig. 81)*—only New York examples of this apparently serviceable form are known. Its handle is in the early New York style. Van Dyck's chafing dish (in the Museum of the City of New York) is probably a transition piece; its shape is found in the later period, while the fleur-de-lis piercing has a bold-

ness and insistent rhythm found in Baroque silver. It should be compared with the early Philadelphia chafing dishes *(see Fig. 82)* by Johannis Nys (1671–1734).

Surviving Philadelphia silver of the Baroque period consists mainly of trifid-end spoons and porringers. Four silversmiths were active in this and the succeeding period in the rapidly growing city—Johannis Nys, Francis Richardson (1681–1729), Cesar Ghiselin (1670–1734), and Philip Syng, Sr. (1676–1739). Nys is best remembered for his tankards with repeated, stamped bands of leaves above the baseband, in the New York manner, and for a rare and charming pair of chafing dishes *(Fig. 82)* with scrolled feet, hornlike bracket supports, and boldly pierced fleur-de-lis patterns on the sides. Syng's silver is rare; best known are his copies of an English flagon and basin that had been presented to Christ Church, Philadelphia, by Queen Anne in 1708 (which may have provided Philadelphians with their first glimpse of silver in the new plain style). Syng's copies are dated 1712.

Spoons—always fairly numerous compared to hollow ware—underwent a change in the Baroque period. The trifid end of the 1690's *(see Fig. 28)* grew less strongly delineated and became known as the wavy end; the oval bowl had a plain rattail (a solid V-shaped ornament in relief). Spoons were generally made in three sizes—tablespoon, teaspoon, and an intermediate size. New York makers continued to make their caryatid-handle spoons into the first quarter of the eighteenth century.

80. Mustard pot, *ca.* 1700–1715, by Peter van Dyck; H. 5⅛ inches. Yale University Art Gallery, New Haven, Connecticut. The Mabel Brady Garvan Collection.

81. Covered porringer, *ca.* 1705–20, by Peter van Dyck; L. 7¹⁵⁄₁₆ inches. Yale University Art Gallery, New Haven, Connecticut. The Mabel Brady Garvan Collection.

82

---

82. Pair of chafing dishes, *ca.* 1700–1720, by Johannis Nys; L. 14¾ inches. Philadelphia Museum of Art. Bequest of R. Wistar Harvey (Acc. no. 40-16-700) and given by Mr. and Mrs. Elliston P. Morris (Acc. no. 67-209-1).

83. Teapot, *ca.* 1715–22, by John Coney; H. 7⅜ inches. The Metropolitan Museum of Art, New York. Bequest of A. T. Clearwater, 1933.

CHAPTER FOUR

83

Queen Anne Silver

Years of peace brought a burgeoning trade and an ever expanding economy to the colonial cities in the second quarter of the eighteenth century. As the population grew and the cities expanded physically, so that part of society which valued intellectual and cultural things grew more mature and more ambitious. This is inevitably reflected in the arts of the early Rococo period.

By about 1750, Boston housed more than twice as many inhabitants as it had at the end of the seventeenth century: over sixteen thousand. New York's population multiplied almost three times in these years, to eleven thousand, to be exceeded by Philadelphia with thirteen thousand. As a corollary, the cities increased in size geographically, with much building of houses, streets, bridges, and public places. New wharves, docks and ships, shops and warehouses signaled the prospering state of commerce. Suburbs grew up around Philadelphia, while the city outskirts were

91

distinguished by large estates with formal Italian gardens, indicative of a rich society. Here, master builders formed the Carpenters Company to obtain instruction in the science of architecture, which certainly contributed to the superior quality of the new brick Christ Church, Assembly Building, and State House—some of the finest architecture in the colonies at this time.

By-products of commercial prosperity appeared in surplus capital available for investment, specialized business services, and the beginnings of modern credit. Developing trade brought demands for improved communications with rural areas surrounding the cities. Manufacturing enterprises were sufficiently successful to induce an element of apprehension in English competitors. An unusually wide range of consumer goods, exotic and otherwise, became available in the cities; milliners, haberdashers, spectacle-makers, cosmetic shops, and ornamental marble carvers thrived. Holland stoves and wallpaper, tinglazed earthenware (Delft), and glass of the latest fashion were all constantly in demand for elegant houses with an abundance of servants, coaches, and trappings. Tea services of gold were not unknown in the richest families. London merchants sent their newest merchandise to the colonies, and many an English gentleman sought a rich, and obviously socially acceptable, consort on American shores.

As religious faiths expanded and old bigotries disappeared, so new and ever more handsome churches were built. Plays, concerts, balls, and assemblies proliferated, and clubs of all kinds and degrees of exclusiveness sprang up. Not all was frivolity, however, for groups of intellectuals in Boston and Philadelphia particularly displayed a marked scientific curiosity. Numerous bookshops did a thriving business, and there were two or more regular newspapers in each major city. The English painter John Smibert

arrived in New England in this period and soon established a studio in Boston. Several painters, immigrant and native, whose works have survived in part practiced in the cities—notably Peter Pelham and Joseph Badger in Boston, and Robert Feke and Gustavus Hesselius in Philadelphia. Furniture of these areas also achieved a rare degree of excellence in this early Rococo style.

As life in the colonies of this period exhibits a progressive economic growth and increasing self-confidence, so the silver manifests a sureness and lack of ostentation that marks some of the loveliest objects ever made in America. Instead of the emphatic concern with ornamentation, with a vital movement and a rich façade characteristic of the William and Mary period, silversmiths in the second quarter of the eighteenth century were preoccupied almost exclusively with formal values, as their English colleagues had been for the previous decade.

Much has been made in the past of the dominating role of the "Britannia Standard" in this development: Fear of a shortage of coinage resulting from the enormous demand for plate caused Parliament in 1697 to raise the price of the raw material and also raise the percentage of pure silver in plate. This, it is claimed, made the silver softer (because there was less copper to harden the alloy) and therefore more difficult to work; thus, silversmiths preferred plain objects rather than highly elaborate ones. The fallacy of the argument is that Parliament passed this act on the eve, as we have seen, of the most elaborate period of silver so far. It is impossible to believe that the act would not have been enforced in the colonies for another twenty years, which is the time elapsing before the introduction of the plainer forms. As English historians have noted, and as mentioned here already, plain styles were popular even in the periods of the greatest enrichment of silver, and their dominance in the Queen Anne period was due as much to a continuing preference as a reaction against the elaboration of Baroque styles.

Early Rococo styles seem to have been introduced into America by the numerous royal gifts of ecclesiastical silver that followed the spread of Anglicanism in the colonies. Although no royal silver of this period has survived from the Boston churches, it is significant that the earliest datable American piece of Queen Anne silver was given in 1714 to the Anglican New North Church. (Made by John Dixwell, it is now in King's Chapel, Boston, and is very similar to the two-handled cup illustrated in Figure 113.) Yet, as we have seen, Baroque silver of the William and Mary style stayed in fashion until the 1720's.

John Coney continued to dominate Boston silversmithing at the beginning of this period. Although he died in 1722 at the advanced age (for that time) of sixty-six, he made several masterpieces in the new style. One of the earliest of these, and perhaps the earliest example of its form in Boston, was a teapot engraved with the Mascarène arms in a typical Queen Anne scroll-and-acanthus cartouche *(Fig. 83)*. Of a bulbous pear-shape—a form that typifies this period, although, as we shall see, subject to development from this early example—and undecorated except for the engraving and the slight molding at the lip and on the lower part of the spout, the teapot obviously derives from the kind of form seen in Figure 33. Aesthetically, the emphasis lies in the inherent beauty of the material and on the sinuous Rococo "line of beauty"—the Hogarthian term for a line that curves and reverse-curves in three dimensions; on this piece, it may be drawn from the lip of the body downward, going around the body as it descends. Its well-known counterpart in furniture of this period is the cabriole leg, while the emphasis placed on the actual material may be compared with the cabinetmaker's use of beautifully grained, solid walnut. Although the proportions of this object are disfigured by a replaced handle, and the character of the piece may be summarized as robust rather than lovely, it is an important early work.

The plain bell-shape of the body of Coney's two-handled cup, engraved with the Flynt arms and dated 1718 *(Fig. 84)*, can be seen on the smaller Dixwell piece already mentioned *(see Fig. 113)*. However, a comparison with Coney's earlier Stoughton cup and Winslow's two-handled cup *(see Figs. 47 and 48)* should also be made. The cup stands on a high splayed foot, has a domed cover with finial, and two hollow scroll handles. Manifest is the silversmith's attention to surface and to curvilinear forms. The curve of the handles (scroll or cabriole form) repeats the curve of the lower part of the body, and the molding of the cover recalls the stepped molding of the foot, a motif that is repeated in slightly changed form in the finial. The architectural, scrolled elements in the cartouche are also part of this vocabulary of forms.

Compared to the candlesticks by Kierstede *(see Fig. 56)*, the pair by John Burt (1693–1746) illustrated here are small and plain indeed *(Fig. 85)*. But in no way does this compromise the sheer loveliness of their profile and proportions. Of an octagonal form, which became popular in the first years of the century and was brought to perfection in this period, they combine straight lines and curves superbly. This is what makes them so beautiful: the flaring and narrowing of each surface up and down the baluster stem (a cabriole in profile) and the subtle, sculpted movement of each facet of the foot as it moves up to the first knop of the stem. Although they resemble the examples by Winslow *(see Fig. 70)* and Coney, their marvelous fluidity is so different from the polygonal faceting and geometric harmony of the

84

84. Two-handled covered cup, *ca.* 1718, by John Coney; H. 10 inches. Courtesy of R. W. Norton Art Gallery, Shreveport, Louisiana.

85. Pair of candlesticks, 1724, by John Burt; H. 7 inches. Fogg Art Museum, Harvard University, Cambridge, Massachusetts.

85

earlier pairs. The candlesticks were given to tutor Nicholas Sever of Harvard College by his pupils in 1724. Several fine pieces by Burt were given to this popular teacher and have been preserved.

Although the pear-shape is so typical of this period (we have already discussed it in connection with the early teapot by Coney), it was rarely used for New England teapots; only two or three examples survive. The more characteristic New England form is seen in the excellent example *(Fig. 86)* by Jacob Hurd (1703–58). There is, however, at least a fifteen-year gap between Coney's piece and Hurd's (the latter was a presentation piece dated 1737). Indeed, there are few Boston teapots earlier than this—an inexplicable fact. Distinguished by its rotund, apple-shaped body, a splayed foot that raises it sufficiently from the ground, and an elegant spout—ten-sided below, with a baluster drop at the juncture with the body—this fine piece is further embellished with an engraved band round the lid and the Henchman arms in an elegant scroll-and-acanthus cartouche with scaled ground

on the side. The lid is inset and disguised so that it does not interrupt the profile. The accompanying sugar bowl occupies a different world from the previous sugar containers we have seen *(see Figs. 49 and 50)*. Although at first glance a simple object, it is in fact a virtuoso piece, a complex series of variations on the Rococo line—foot and bowl, bowl and cover, cover and handle, foot and cover handle. These relationships, it must be remembered, are also established in depth. Cartouche and crest have been adapted to the different shape of the sugar bowl, and are fine examples of engraving.

Also globular or apple-shaped in form is the monumental teakettle on stand *(Fig. 87)* by Jacob Hurd. It is the earliest complete example known in American silver, and is engraved with the Lowell arms. Large areas of plain surface unite with the sinuous curves of spout and handle, whose movement is repeated and intensified in the cabriole legs and brackets of the stand. It is the precious material and the elegant line that invite admiration. Comparison of the spout with that on the

86

87

86. Teapot and sugar bowl, 1737, by Jacob Hurd; H. (teapot) 5¾ inches. Courtesy of Museum of Fine Arts, Boston. Spalding Collection.

87. Teakettle on stand, *ca.* 1725–35, by Jacob Hurd; H. 14⅜ inches. Private collection. Photograph courtesy of Museum of Fine Arts, Boston.

earlier kettle by Kierstede *(see Fig. 78)* reveals the difference in attitude between the Baroque and the early Rococo. In its massiveness and rarity it is a highly important object.

Monumental and also beautiful, of extraordinary felicity of shape and line, the two-handled covered cup by Jacob Hurd is surely the apogee of Queen Anne silver *(Fig. 88)*. Appropriately called a "bishop" in contemporary descriptions, it is one of the largest and heaviest pieces of American silver of this century, weighing almost six pounds and standing over fifteen inches high. It was subscribed for by a group of Boston merchants and presented to Edward Tyng, the captain of a small vessel that captured the first French privateer in "King George's War" in 1744; as such, it symbolizes the pride of Boston society at this time.

Its development from the Coney cup *(see Fig. 84)*, made at the beginning of this period, is obvious. The main differences are in the increased elevation of foot and cover, the insertion of a high collar between foot and body, and the addition of a midband on the body above the lower handle junctures. This band serves to articulate the expanse of the sides of the body. The molding on foot and cover are virtually identical and immediately create a marked rhythm, which the strong midband reinforces. The elaboration of the handles—ridges at the sides, the molded collar at the top junctures, and the strut at the lower—increases the impression of richness. The finial, in its bold outline and intricate detail, crowns the form. As a final enrichment, the engraved decoration consists of an inscription within a sinuous Rococo cartouche surrounded by a lavish trophy of arms.

It has been noted that the cup conveys an impression of great height. Compared to the still primarily horizontal proportions of the Coney and Winslow cups of the Baroque period *(see Figs. 47 and 48)*,

this cup is vertical in axis. The development is a gradual one, however, for here width and height (excluding finial) are identical: it is the finial that adds the flourish and provides the vertical accent.

Hurd's control of what is a very large object was masterly. Indeed, the piece has architectonic qualities, recalling the facade of a great house in its articulation (splendid homes such as Westover, Virginia, were being built in this period). The foot calls to mind the front steps; the body the main building with its string courses and its sharply pitched roof, crowned by chimney; the handles the recessed wings.

Pear-shaped teapots were more common in New York than in New England in the Queen Anne period. Only one remains, however, with the octagonal variation *(Fig. 89)*. Its intricate use of plain surfaces and moldings recalls the Burt candlesticks *(see Fig. 85)*, although its outline has a more intense rhythm. The curve and reverse-curve of the neck and spout (which is also octagonal), the handle, and the belly proclaim its stylistic origin, while the facets emphasize the preciousness of the material. Comparison should also be made with two other excellent pyriform teapots by this maker, Peter van Dyck *(see Figs. 95 and 96)*, to underline the qualities of richness and intensity that so distinguish this object.

Huguenot silversmiths are generally credited with introducing the cut-card ornament into England and consequently into America. Its use in New York is seen in the work of those craftsmen of French origin or training, such as Van Dyck and Charles Le Roux (1689–1745). In Boston

---

88. Two-handled covered cup, 1744, by Jacob Hurd; H. 15⅛ inches. Yale University Art Gallery, New Haven, Connecticut. The Mabel Brady Garvan Collection.

89

89. Teapot, *ca.* 1720–35, by Peter van Dyck; H. 7⅛ inches. Yale University Art Gallery, New Haven, Connecticut. The Mabel Brady Garvan Collection.

90. Two-handled covered cup, *ca.* 1730, by Charles Le Roux; 10¼ inches. Yale University Art Gallery, New Haven, Connecticut. The Mabel Brady Garvan Collection.

it appeared in the previous period, while in New York it became popular mainly at this time. Le Roux's work is of excellent quality, and two of his objects are among the masterpieces of the period. His two-handled cup *(Fig. 90)* made for the De Peyster family is rare and unusual, since it has cut-card ornament on both body and cover, and harp-shaped handles —a kind seldom used in America. These handles, which are also ridged and fluted, strongly emphasize the scroll form and reverse-curves of the style. Formal and decorative balances, in the foot-and-cover shape and in the ornament, play an important role, while the midband is placed high to accommodate the high cut-card ornament on the body. The cartouche is similar in form to that on the Coney cup *(see Fig. 84).*

Charles Le Roux's coffeepot *(Fig. 91)* is a superlative example of emphasis on sheer line and proportion, and deliberate lack of ornament. It is rare to find a coffeepot of this period with the handle placed at right angles to the spout (it is doubtful that it was intended for chocolate, since it lacks the removable finial). Yet this juxtaposition undoubtedly enhances the form. The taper of the body is echoed in the spout (whose rounded form

100

is also recalled in the disk at the juncture), while the subtle curves of the cover are repeated in the handle. The marked geometric outline and the brilliance of the material convey a vivid impression of strength and delicacy, of practicality and elegance.

It is impossible to ignore the exceptional beauty of New York silver of this period, or deny its extraordinary felicity of line and proportion. The synthesis was achieved most perfectly, perhaps, in the work of Simeon Soumain (1685–1750), especially in two small but quite masterful objects illustrated here. The sugar caster *(Fig. 92)* engraved with the Maddox arms has the octagonal shape we have already seen on the Van Dyck teapot, united with the baluster form typical of Queen Anne casters. Again, it is proportion that distinguishes the piece—the relation of belly width to body height, the height of the foot, the width of the neck, the commanding height of the cover. Again, it is the curve and reverse-curve, the expanding and narrowing of the facets that so attracts the eye, with the marked rhythms of molded foot, midband, cover flange, and finial.

In contrast to these rhythms, the sugar

bowl gives an impression of extraordinary fluidity *(Fig. 93)*. Not the defined contrasts of the octagonal baluster here, but the smooth transitions of Rococo line and circle: footring and matching cover-ring, the expanded circle of the lip, the slightly narrower cover rim, the border of the engraved cipher on the body, slightly diminished when repeated on the cover. The molding of the footring and the cover-ring seem to provide exactly the right contrast to the plain surfaces. It may well be the outstanding example in American silver of a graceful profile, at once languid and contained.

This bowl should be compared to the Boston sugar bowl previously illustrated *(see Fig. 86)*. Here are two examples of a form common to this period, based on Chinese porcelain forms. Yet the Soumain piece undoubtedly conveys better the qualities of preciousness and delicacy that porcelain evoked, while the Hurd bowl has a broader, squatter profile. There is also this contrast in the engraving: The Henchman arms on the Boston piece appear in the traditional strong shield and cartouche, while the letters EC (for Elizabeth Cruger) on the New York piece become a fanciful cipher of circular swirls and flourishes that harmonize more fully with the form of the bowl.

One of the earliest great Philadelphia pieces was made presumably at the end of the Queen Anne period *(Fig. 94)*, for it utilizes a double-scroll handle that is generally seen on fully developed Rococo silver. This massive tankard by Philip

91. Coffeepot, *ca.* 1720–35, by Charles Le Roux; H. 10¾ inches. Yale University Art Gallery, New Haven, Connecticut. The Mabel Brady Garvan Collection.

92. Caster, *ca.* 1725–40, by Simeon Soumain; H. 7⅜ inches. Yale University Art Gallery, New Haven, Connecticut. The Mabel Brady Garvan Collection.

92

103

Syng, Jr. (1703–89) has a very marked English character in its broadness, its slight foot (instead of a baseband), and its strongly domed cover. The molded midband serves the same purpose on this object as it does on the great Hurd cup (see Fig. 88). Engraved on the front is an elaborate version of the Maddox arms, with architectural elements, human figures, and animals in the cartouche. The molding on the cover recalls that on the foot, while the extra scroll on the lower part of the handle adds a further flourish, as does the curved base of the body. Instead of applied swags or lions on the handle, Syng here chose a rattail motif. It is one of the grandest of all American tankards.

Changing social habits brought a different range of silver forms into popularity in the Queen Anne period. The newly fashionable luxury of drinking tea was responsible for a greatly increased number of silver teapots and sugar bowls (the liquid was presumably imbibed from Chinese porcelain or Delft teacups). This fashion also inspired a new range of furniture forms, such as tea tables with elegant cabriole legs. Pear-shaped teapots were immensely popular in New York but hardly at all in Boston; the latter city preferred the apple-shaped pots that do not appear to have been made in New York. Few teapots of Philadelphia manufacture have survived from this period.

An early form of teapot by Peter van Dyck, with a lovely, languid profile, epitomizes early Rococo silver (Fig. 95). The virtually uninterrupted surface gives a fluid quality to the linear design. Comparison with a later and more typical New

York teapot by the same maker (Fig. 96) is instructive. The later example makes plentiful use of molded ornament—on the foot, at the contraflexure of the body, at the lip, and on the cover, while the spout is octagonal rather than plain, recalling the geometrical molding. Many New York silversmiths made examples of this handsome form.

Although the earliest Boston teapots were pear-shaped (see Fig. 83), very few examples remain. Most surviving teapots from that city appear to date from the mid-1730's and early 1740's, and present slight variations on the beautiful apple-shape (see Fig. 86). Boston silversmiths frequently varied the form of the spout, however; another example by Hurd (Fig. 97) has a plainer and less striking spout than his earlier example. This piece is engraved with arms and cartouche that bear vivid witness to his skill. A similar, smaller example by Joseph Richardson of Philadelphia (1711–84) is known (in the Metropolitan Museum).

Small bowl-shaped containers for sugar were common in the second quarter of the eighteenth century. Most of these closely resemble the form already illustrated (see Figs. 86 and 93), although few attain the superb proportions of the Soumain example. An attractive version can be seen in a sugar bowl by Paul Revere, Sr. (1702–54), father of the most famous of all American silversmiths (Fig. 98). Revere, Sr., had started his career as an apprentice to John Coney, and the use of a regular engraved ornament on the cover of this example recalls Baroque styles. As a further variation, such silversmiths as Hurd and Richardson turned to the octagonal shape (Fig. 99); slightly elongated, it presents a graceful outline and a handsome form.

The earliest cream jugs appeared in this period, as a necessary part of the tea service. Utilizing the pear-shaped body that was also common for cups and canns

94. Tankard, *ca.* 1725–40, by Philip Syng, Jr.; H. 8⅝ inches. Yale University Art Gallery, New Haven, Connecticut. The Mabel Brady Garvan Collection.

95. Teapot, *ca.* 1715–25, by Peter van Dyck; H. 7¾ inches. Yale University Art Gallery, New Haven, Connecticut. The Mabel Brady Garvan Collection.

96. Teapot, *ca.* 1720–40, by Peter van Dyck; H. 7 inches. Yale University Art Gallery, New Haven, Connecticut. The Mabel Brady Garvan Collection.

(that is, pyriform mugs) at this time, the few known examples are set on a splayed foot similar to that on sugar bowls. A small solid handle is applied to the side of the jug, and occasionally a hinged cover above. John Edwards and Jacob Hurd made this form in Boston. Its successor, surviving in greater quantities, had a longer body, usually formed with a serrated rim and a longer pouring lip, and set on three cabriole legs. The example by Hurd shown here is highly unusual in its ornate decoration *(Fig. 100);* three reserves on the sides contain engraved representations of pastoral scenes and a view of Fort Castle William.

A few tea caddies have survived from the Queen Anne period, mainly from New York. An example by Simeon Soumain in the Metropolitan Museum *(Fig. 101)* is fully English in style. It is octagonal in form with a high domed cover and an engraving of the Bayard arms in an appropriate cartouche *(see Fig. 12).*

The Queen Anne chocolate or coffeepot by Charles Le Roux already discussed *(see Fig. 91)* appears to be unique in form. One of the earliest coffeepots of the period was made by Coney *(Fig. 102).* Essentially an elongated pear-shape, it has a stepped, domed cover and splayed foot, a wooden scroll handle and spout similar to that seen previously on teakettles. Much more typical of the period is the late but

97

98   99

beautiful example *(Fig. 103)* by Zachariah Brigden (1734–87). With its straight-tapered body, well-defined base molding, elaborate molding at the juncture of body and octagonal spout (which is opposite the handle), and elegant domed cover, this coffeepot has a finely proportioned form. It bears a Rococo version of engraved arms typical of the ensuing period.

The ever handsome tankard form underwent certain changes in these years. Boston makers enhanced it with a domed

---

97. Teapot, *ca.* 1730–45, by Jacob Hurd; H. 5⅛ inches. Yale University Art Gallery, New Haven, Connecticut. The Mabel Brady Garvan Collection.

98. Sugar bowl, *ca.* 1725–40, by Paul Revere, Sr.; H. 4¾ inches. The Heritage Foundation, Old Deerfield, Massachusetts.

99. Sugar bowl, *ca.* 1740–50, by Jacob Hurd; H. 4⅜ inches. Courtesy of Museum of Fine Arts, Boston. Charles H. Tyler Fund.

cover and, slightly later, with a midband, in addition to making the body taller and slimmer *(Fig. 104)*. Thumbpieces were changed into the scroll type, a finial was generally added to the top of the cover, and terminals assumed a disk form, frequently with a cast mask applied. Furthermore, there was often a disk at the lower handle juncture and a shaped pendent drop on the body from the upper juncture. Base moldings also differed from their predecessors *(see Fig. 63)*. A feature that appeared late in the Queen Anne period and continued into the third quarter of the century was a turned-down cover flange.

New York tankards of the Queen Anne period were quite different *(Fig. 105)*. Rarely domed or with finial, covers generally remained flat; frequently a foreign coin was inserted into the cover or used as a terminal. Gone was the earlier New York motif of the repeated, stamped band

100

101

102

110

of leaves at the base, and the baseband, too, was changed. The body remained comparatively short and broad; consequently the handle did not achieve the slim, elegant scroll shape of the best Boston examples. Thumbpieces were either scrolled or of the corkscrew variety, and there was frequently an appliqué of naturalistic or geometrical forms on the handle.

Philadelphia tankards that survive from this period generally present a heavier appearance than those from the other two cities *(Fig. 106)*. The drum is low and broad, frequently with a midband, and the cover is domed without a finial. The baseband is often similar to that on New York tankards. Examples by members of the Richardson and Syng family are known. One exceptional tankard, by

100. Cream jug, *ca.* 1730–45, by Jacob Hurd; H. 4 inches. Yale University Art Gallery, New Haven, Connecticut. The Mabel Brady Garvan Collection.

101. Tea caddy, *ca.* 1725–40, by Simeon Soumain; H. 4⁷⁄₁₆ inches. The Metropolitan Museum of Art, New York. Gift of E. M. Newlin, 1964.

102. Coffeepot, *ca.* 1715–22, by John Coney; H. 9⁵⁄₁₆ inches. Courtesy of Museum of Fine Arts, Boston. Anonymous loan.

103. Coffeepot, *ca.* 1760–70, by Zachariah Brigden; H. 9⅞ inches. Courtesy of Museum of Fine Arts, Boston.

103

William Vilant (*ca.* 1725), was finely engraved by Joseph Leddel of New York in 1750; scenes from Ovid cover the entire surface of the drum (Heritage Foundation, Deerfield, Massachusetts).

Smaller drinking vessels of this period, straight-sided and without covers, were called mugs. First introduced in the preceding period, these vessels were generally plain and had a tapered strap handle, which was soon replaced by the hollow type such as that on the tankard. Boston mugs were generally quite plain with a baseband similar to that on tankards, with or without a high midband, and frequently lacking the tankard's specially shaped applied handle terminal. The end of the handle could be curved up and the upper surface assume an undulating shape *(Fig. 107)*. New York mugs were often rich in appearance *(Fig. 108)*, with a complex midband and occasionally the repeated, stamped band of leaves at the base typical of the earlier periods. Even the applied handle ornament common on

111

104

105

106

107

104. Tankard, *ca.* 1745, by John Burt; H. 8¼ inches. Yale University Art Gallery, New Haven, Connecticut. The Mabel Brady Garvan Collection.

105. Tankard, *ca.* 1730–40, by Simeon Soumain; H. 6⁵⁄₁₆ inches. Collection of Mrs. Edsel B. Ford, Grosse Pointe Shores, Michigan.

106. Tankard, *ca.* 1730–40, by Francis Richardson; H. 7 inches. Philadelphia Museum of Art. Lent by Dr. Isaac Starr.

107. Mug, *ca.* 1715–22, by John Coney; H. 4⅛ inches. Yale University Art Gallery, New Haven, Connecticut. The Mabel Brady Garvan Collection.

New York tankards was transferred to mugs.

By the middle of the Queen Anne period, mug bodies changed from tapered to pyriform, and are known as canns. The earliest Boston examples had a distinctive shape—not truly pyriform, but as if a slight bulge had been added to the lower part of an otherwise straight-sided vessel *(Fig. 109)*. Later the neck of such vessels was more pinched in and the lip given greater flare. New York makers were also slow to utilize the pear-shape for canns. The earliest type *(Fig. 110)* is only slightly narrowed at the bottom, the sides only slightly curved, and the lip simply flared. The example illustrated here was made probably in the 1730's by Jacob Ten Eyck of Albany, and utilizes the double-scroll handle normally associated with the ensuing period. Yet the handsome Douw coat of arms is surrounded by a swirling Baroque-type cartouche. Not until the fully developed Rococo period do we find the pear-shape freely used by New York makers for canns and tankards.

A superb example of the Queen Anne flagon is that by John Potwine (1698–1792), who moved from Boston to Connecticut in this period *(Fig. 111)*. Many of the details that distinguish early Rococo tankards—domed cover, finial, scroll thumbpiece, body drop—can be seen here. A handsome cartouche in the Queen Anne style *(Fig. 112)* is engraved on the front of this imposing object, which was given to the First Parish Church of Charlestown, Massachusetts, in the 1720's.

Important Queen Anne two-handled cups have already been discussed *(see Figs. 84 and 88)*. Variations on these types consisted mainly in the placement of the midband and details of the handles. Another, less monumental, type of cup, is epitomized by an example *(Fig. 113)* by John Dixwell (1680–1725), which was given in 1717 to the same church as the flagon just mentioned. It is one of the earliest forms of Queen Anne silver known in America; in essence, it is a beaker with two simple, widely scrolled strap handles added. The beaker proper is in evidence throughout the period. The example by Jacob Hurd shown here *(Fig. 114)* was made for the Rehoboth Church in 1747, thirty years later than the Dixwell cup,

108

109

110

and is beautifully engraved with appropriate inscription within a scrolled frame.

Simple bowls set on footrings appeared in this period in Boston and New York. Generally small—about six inches in diameter—they were often plain, lacking even an engraved inscription. They were probably used with the tea service (as a slop bowl), though it is also possible that they were used for rinsing fingers at the dinner table. An exceptional bowl of this period is the only known Queen Anne Monteith *(Fig. 115);* as one might have expected, this rare object was made by John Coney. It offers a valuable comparison to his earlier, highly elaborate Monteith *(see Fig. 51).* Its unadorned surfaces, the undulating curves of the rim (which is detachable so that the bowl may also be used as a conventional punch bowl), the engraved cartouche, all typify this period. Made for the Livingston family of New York, it is an unusual example of an important piece commissioned from a Boston silver-

108. Mug, *ca.* 1710-25, by Simeon Soumain; H. 3⅞ inches. Yale University Art Gallery, New Haven, Connecticut. The Mabel Brady Garvan Collection.

109. Cann, *ca.* 1715–25, by William Pollard; H. 5¼ inches. Yale University Art Gallery, New Haven, Connecticut. The John Marshall Phillips Collection.

110. Cann, *ca.* 1730–40, by Jacob Ten Eyck; H. 4 inches. The Metropolitan Museum of Art, New York. Gift of Mrs. Abraham Lansing, 1901.

115

111

112

113

114

smith by a prominent New York family. It lacks the excellent proportions and splendid virtuosity of Coney's earlier Colman Monteith.

Chafing dishes in the early Rococo style *(Fig. 116)* appear much more graceful than their predecessors. The bowl became less straight-sided, and the reel-shaped appendage on the bottom less prominent. Piercing took the form of small, graceful scrolls, often intermingled with vertical slots. Legs grew slimmer and generally

---

111. Flagon, *ca.* 1720–30, by John Potwine; H. 13⅝ inches. Yale University Art Gallery, New Haven, Connecticut. The Mabel Brady Garvan Collection.

112. Arms and inscription. Detail of Fig. 111.

113. Two-handled cup, *ca.* 1717, by John Dixwell; H. 6¹¹⁄₁₆ inches: Yale University Art Gallery, New Haven, Connecticut. The Mabel Brady Garvan Collection.

114. Beaker, 1747, by Jacob Hurd; H. 5¹³⁄₁₆ inches. Yale University Art Gallery, New Haven, Connecticut. The Mabel Brady Garvan Collection.

115

115. Monteith bowl, *ca.* 1715–22, by John Coney; D. 11⅝ inches. Franklin D. Roosevelt Library, Hyde Park, New York.

116. Chafing dish, *ca.* 1725–40, by Jacob Hurd; H. 3⅝ inches. Yale University Art Gallery, New Haven, Connecticut. The Mabel Brady Garvan Collection.

117. Trencher salt, *ca.* 1720–30, by Philip Syng, Sr.; L. 3 inches. Philadelphia Museum of Art. Purchased: Temple Fund (Acc. no. 23-33-1).

116

117

terminated either in a claw, which was meant to cover a ball made of wood for insulating purposes (this motif was introduced in silver long before the ball-and-claw foot appeared in furniture), or in a hoof, as in this example by Jacob Hurd made for the Henchman family of Boston. This piece originally had a silver socket for a turned wooden handle on one of the legs. Coney made five versions of the ball-and-claw-footed chafing dishes. Surprisingly, the form does not seem to have been so popular in New York or Philadelphia.

Some of the most charming silver forms of these years are those intended for the dispensing of condiments—salts, pepper boxes, mustard pots, and sugar casters. Although small, they often have attractive proportions and exquisite detail that fully betoken the silversmiths' art and skill. Salts in trencher form survive from the beginning of this period. An octagonal version by Philip Syng, Sr., of Philadelphia, illustrated here *(Fig. 117)*, recalls the elongated form of the octagonal sugar bowl by Hurd *(see Fig. 99)*. Later in the period, bowl-like salts on three cabriole legs, with trifid, or pad feet, grew popular.

An exception to the general plainness of these is an intricately detailed pair of very beautiful workmanship by Charles Le Roux *(Fig. 118);* here the legs are in the form of dolphins surmounted by mermaid masks. On the sides, between the masks, are applied swags of fruit.

Pepper boxes and casters are frequently delightful objects. Often octagonal, the boxes are generally tapered from a splayed baseband to an identically shaped rim molding. Covers are domed and pierced and often have finials, while a simple strap handle is applied to one face. The example here *(Fig. 119)* by Paul Revere, Sr., shows the earlier type with a slightly bulbous cover that later became slimmer and often taller. The pepper box was popular at the beginning of the Queen Anne period, but was later replaced by the caster.

A superb early hexagonal caster by Coney is one of the few faceted Boston examples known *(Fig. 120)*. The bold curve of the body and the striking stepped foot provide ample support for the tall, domed, elegantly pierced cover. Engraved with the Charnock arms, it is a small masterpiece. Later silversmiths employed an

118

119

118. Pair of salts, *ca.* 1720–40, by Charles Le Roux; H. 1⅞ inches. The Metropolitan Museum of Art, New York. Dodge Fund, 1935.

119. Pepper box, *ca.* 1725–35, by Paul Revere, Sr.; H. 3½ inches. Worcester Art Museum, Worcester, Massachusetts. Gift of Frances M. Lincoln.

120. Caster, *ca.* 1715–22, by John Coney; H. 6¼ inches. Courtesy of Museum of Fine Arts, Boston. Gift of Mr. and Mrs. Francis S. Dane.

121. Caster, 1765, by Joseph Edwards, Jr.; H. 5⅜ inches. Yale University Art Gallery, New Haven, Connecticut. The Mabel Brady Garvan Collection.

---

elongated pear-form for casters, which subsequently became the baluster form *(Fig. 121).*

Salvers or trays in this period were generally fashioned with bracket supports or cabriole legs rather than the earlier trumpet foot. The outline also changed from the simple round form (with occasional variations) of the preceding period to a boldly defined, almost architectural configuration, as illustrated by Hurd's masterpiece for the Clarke family *(Fig. 122).* While the molded edge of this tray is Baroque in its strong rhythms, the outline of the band of engraved decoration inside the edge gives a sinuous Rococo move-

121

ment to the piece. Furthermore, the cartouche has a delicate, fanciful Rococo aspect.

As smooth and graceful as the Hurd example is vigorous, the salver by Charles Le Roux *(Fig. 123)* is based on Chinese forms, as is the Soumain sugar bowl *(see Fig. 93)*. In its emphasis on line rather than ornament, its exquisite proportions and superior workmanship, it exemplifies the best qualities of the early Rococo.

Among the rarities of American silver, candlesticks are striking forms. Early in this period, Coney made a pair of distinctive outline, based on the baluster form *(Fig. 124)*. They lack the clear profile of

122

the later style *(Fig. 125)*, also based on the baluster. This type was popular in New York, and several pairs have survived. Those illustrated here are by the great silversmith Charles Le Roux. Identical in all respects to contemporary English examples, they combine the octagon and the baluster to great effect.

Even rarer than the candlesticks in this

123

period are unique, important, or beautiful objects such as the inkstand made by Coney for Jonathan Belcher, governor of Massachusetts and later New Jersey (in the Metropolitan Museum); three small, round containers stand on a triangular plate, which is supported at each corner by a finely modeled *lion couchant*. A lovely pair of sauceboats, a form that first appeared during these years but reached its peak in the following period, by Charles Le Roux, is also rare. Again fully English in form, the long, oval body with scrolled rim stands on a high, splayed foot. It has a pouring lip at each end and a scrolled handle on each side at the center (Philadelphia Museum).

By the second quarter of the eighteenth century, the spoon handle had changed from the undulating "wavy end" of the late William and Mary period to a rounded, slightly upturned end *(Fig. 126)*; the center of the face of the handle was decorated with a "midrib" running from the end toward the bowl. As the period progressed, this midrib tended to get

122. Salver, *ca.* 1725–40, by Jacob Hurd; D. 12⅜ inches. Yale University Art Gallery, New Haven, Connecticut. The Mabel Brady Garvan Collection.

123. Salver, *ca.* 1720–40, by Charles Le Roux; L. 6³⁄₁₆ inches. Yale University Art Gallery, New Haven, Connecticut. The Mabel Brady Garvan Collection.

124. Candlestick, *ca.* 1715–22, by John Coney; H. 6¼ inches. Courtesy of Museum of Fine Arts, Boston. Gift of Mr. and Mrs. D. L. Pickman.

125. Pair of candlesticks, *ca.* 1725–40, by Charles Le Roux; H. 6½ inches. Collection of Mrs. Edsel B. Ford, Grosse Pointe Shores, Michigan.

124

125

126

126. Spoon, *ca.* 1740–50, by Barent Ten Eyck; L. 8⅜ inches. Yale University Art Gallery, New Haven, Connecticut. The Mabel Brady Garvan Collection.

127. Keyhole handle. Detail of a porringer, *ca.* 1740–50, by Paul Revere, Sr.; L. (handle) 2¾ inches. Yale University Art Gallery, New Haven, Connecticut. The William Inglis Morse Collection, gift of his daughter, Mrs. Frederick W. Hilles.

128. Teakettle on stand, *ca.* 1745–55, by Joseph Richardson; H. 15⁵⁄₁₆ inches. Yale University Art Gallery, New Haven, Connecticut. The Mabel Brady Garvan Collection.

127

shorter. The rattail on the back of the bowl was replaced in the two decades before 1750 by a rounded, molded form or drop, sometimes double, or occasionally a shell in relief.

During the second quarter of the century, silversmiths introduced the "keyhole" handle for porringers *(Fig. 127)*. In the first part of the period, there were frequently two arched openings in the porringer handle near the bowl, but these were subsequently discarded. This type, with occasional variations, such as the trefoil opening sometimes found in New York porringer handles, was utilized in the three cities in the Queen Anne period.

124

CHAPTER FIVE

Fully Developed Rococo Silver

Fully developed Rococo styles flourished in the third quarter of the eighteenth century. The period closely resembles the earlier decades that witnessed the full development of Baroque silver, in that extensive warfare between England, France, and Spain (with occasional peaceful interludes) prompted an enormous, if capricious, economic prosperity and physical expansion. Although it exploded in revolution, the period is remarkable for a tenacious devotion to the accumulation and enjoyment of wealth, which manifested itself in all kinds of sophisticated pleasures and activities as well as in the growing number of native craftsmen or "mechanics," some of them of very considerable quality.

Philadelphia's material prominence among the colonial cities increased in this period. By 1775, its forty thousand citizens far exceeded New York's twenty-five thousand and Boston's sixteen thousand. Through its port flowed vast wealth, while its ambitious and intellectually active society made it probably the most elegant and alert provincial city in the British Empire at the time. Its New Building, Market House, and Pennsylvania Hospital rivaled in quality New York's St. George's Chapel and King's College, or Boston's Faneuil Hall and King's Chapel. During this period, too, Peter Harrison designed superb buildings in Newport. King's College (now Columbia University) in New York and Princeton University were founded in these years. The Library Company of Philadelphia expanded enormously at this time, and the Redwood Library was founded in Newport. At the time of the Revolution the three cities supported almost one hundred and fifty bookshops, had sponsored many performances of Baroque music (including Handel's *Messiah*), and patronized a host of establishments retailing all kinds of luxuries.

During these years, colonial society in the three cities was marked by a growing division between the richest merchants, who wished to institute a self-ordained aristocracy, with strict allegiance to the King and the Church of England, and the middle classes, who increasingly cherished notions of political and economic independence. It was mainly the former group that flaunted its wealth ostentatiously; that, for example, caused severe traffic problems on certain occasions with all their carriages; that gave "most sinful feasts," where (the other side of the coin) "the Side Board Range would have put a new Smile upon the Cheeks of Bacchus and his jovial trains"; that developed the kind of "Garden . . . worth 40,000 Pounds. . . . [with] Hot Houses, where things that are tender are put in the winter, and Hot Beds for the West India Fruit." It was mainly this group, widely traveled (often to Europe) but increasingly interbred, that patronized the finest painters to develop their talents in America in this period—John Singleton Copley in Boston and Charles Willson Peale in Philadelphia; and sponsored Benjamin West's travel abroad to further his visual education. Accomplished cabinetmakers, primarily in Boston, Philadelphia, and Newport, received most of their important commissions from this group, as did the highly talented silversmiths Joseph Richardson in Philadelphia, Myer Myers (1723–95) in New York, and Paul Revere (1735–1818) in Boston. These major craftsmen had many gifted colleagues in each city, who appear to have been very adequately supported by society; at the time of the Revolution, approximately fifty silversmiths were advertising frequently in the newspapers of Philadelphia and New York. In contrast to earlier periods, the amount of silver that was made for or has survived in churches is negligible compared to that made and consistently used for purely domestic purposes.

Intricate, asymmetrical decoration, laid

on the sinuous forms that had appeared in the second quarter of the eighteenth century, characterizes fully developed Rococo silver. Exuberance, fantasy, and bountiful rhythms were relished for their own sake. If the word "Rococo" implied extensive use of the shell motif, it meant no less the frequent utilization of other naturalistic forms, such as flowers and leaves, which were interspersed with delicate scrolls. The pear-shape fashionable in the preceding period was still widely favored, but inverted (in typical Rococo mode), so that the form appears to burst outward as it rises. An impression of fragility is invoked by heavy, formal areas resting on lighter ones, such as the belly of the traditional pear-shape on the neck. The preference for rich decoration applied to plain forms corresponds, as we have seen, to the developments of the last decade of the seventeenth century.

The earliest known instance of Rococo ornament in American silver occurs on a typical Queen Anne teapot by Jacob Hurd (in the Harrington Collection). This piece is dated 1745, a year later than Hurd's Tyng cup (see Fig. 88), and bears on each side an engraved Rococo shield with an elegant asymmetrical cartouche composed of shells, scrolls, and slender fronds. Hurd had little time to develop elaborate Rococo forms before his retirement, but by the early 1750's, comparable decoration appears to have become widespread on Boston silver. Rococo forms appeared more slowly; Thomas Edwards, who died in 1755, made one of the earliest—an inverted pear-shaped teapot engraved with the Speakman arms in a Rococo cartouche. The same pattern of development took place in Philadelphia and New York.

It was in Philadelphia where the highest attainments of Rococo silver occurred. That enormously rich, sophisticated city patronized and enjoyed the creations of such great silversmiths as Joseph Richardson and his family, and great cabinetmak-ers such as Thomas Affleck during this period. It was there that the most outstanding piece of American Rococo silver was made by Richardson, about 1750 (Fig. 128). Probably inspired by a teakettle from the service ordered from the great London silversmith Paul de Lamerie in 1744 by the Franks family of Philadelphia, this monumental object attains the pinnacle of Rococo artistry in America. It forms the perfect counterpoint to the Boston Queen Anne example by Hurd (see Fig. 87). The inverted pear-shape of the body narrows down to a small footring that fits inside the collar of the stand, while the whole object (over ninety ounces) rests on three very slender ankles above shell feet. The legs of the stand consist of slim scrolls in wide curves, furthering the effect of fragility and asymmetry. Cast decoration of pierced shells and other animal and vegetable forms hangs between each leg, and these motifs are repeated in the bold chasing or repoussé on the body of the kettle. There the decoration is unified by the Rococo scrolls and surrounds the delicate engraving of the Plumstead arms. The richness of the chasing and the lightness of the engraving form a counterplay of decorative motifs (we have already seen the contrast and counterpoint of forms). The heavy spout of bizarre animal form introduces an emphatic element of asymmetry into the design, which the perfect, superb balance of the handle defies. Indeed, the scrolls of the handle are identical to the legs and so preserve the unity of the whole concept. Further decoration, both bold and delicate, appears on the handle junctures, the cover, and on the collar of the stand. This bold, Rococo object is a symphony of sinuous curves and fantastic scrolls in every dimension, of rich and delicate ornament, of mass and void, with an essential, overriding harmony.

Three superb Philadelphia coffeepots illustrated here display the sequence of

130

129. Coffeepot, *ca.* 1745–55, by Philip Syng, Jr.; H. 11⅞ inches. Philadelphia Museum of Art. Purchased: John D. McIlhenny Fund (Acc. no. 66-20-1).

130. Coffeepot, *ca.* 1780–90, by Joseph Lownes; H. 14⅝ inches. Philadelphia Museum of Art. Given by Mr. and Mrs. Percival E. Foerderer (Acc. no. 56-49-1).

132

forms that can be found in this period, as well as the varying types of decoration. The earliest *(Fig. 129)* is by Philip Syng, Jr., and consists essentially of the long, elegant pear-shape we have already seen, distinguished not only by its proportions but also by its fine Rococo decoration. The same scrolls and naturalistic motifs that occur on the Richardson teakettle appear here, but larger in scale and less profuse. One also observes the same contrast between bold chasing on the body and delicate work on the cover. Spout and handle are beautifully drawn and finely unified, with the scroll motifs repeated on each. The ratio of neck width to body width

gives this choice object a further distinction.

As majestic an example of the inverted pyriform as it is possible to find, the coffeepot by Joseph Lownes (worked *ca.* 1780–1816) is notable mainly for its exquisite proportions and restrained decoration *(Fig. 130)*. The ratio of the heights of foot, body, and cover is superb, while the eye is inevitably led from the generous belly of the piece to the sensitive narrowing and slight flare of the neck. If the spout is unusually tall, its comparatively rich decoration unifies it into the total design, while it also balances the handle (again, notice the play of inverted curves). Cover and foot are complementary in shape, as well as in the repetition of the typical Philadelphia beaded ornament which is also seen on the spout. That this pot dates from the end of the Rococo period may be inferred from the character of the engraved decoration, which consists of neoclassical swags and a cipher in the delicate foliate manner of the time.

Probably dating from the 1780's also is the fourth Philadelphia masterpiece shown

131. Coffeepot, *ca.* 1780–90, by Joseph Richardson, Jr. and Nathaniel Richardson; H. 11⅞ inches. Yale University Art Gallery, New Haven, Connecticut. The Mabel Brady Garvan Collection.

132. Cake basket, *ca.* 1755–65, by Myer Myers; L. 14½ inches. The Metropolitan Museum of Art, New York. Morris K. Jesup Fund, 1954.

here, a coffeepot *(Fig. 131)* by two sons of Joseph Richardson—Joseph, Jr., and Nathaniel—working in partnership between 1771 and 1791. Ostensibly simpler than the preceding pots, it is no less remarkable. It is distinguished by extraordinary felicity of line and proportion—the long body slowly expanding to the ample belly, the wide foot, and the elegant cover. Decoration consists of an elaborately chased spout, beading on the foot, which is repeated on the cover, and the Rococo arms and cartouche on the side. Although Philadelphia Rococo is especially noted for the richness of its ornament, it can also, as in this choice object, achieve the uttermost perfection of form and outline.

Rococo silver made in the best tradition of New York silversmithing achieves rare, elegant beauty and delicacy. It is a short step from the distinguished work of Le Roux, Soumain, and Van Dyck in the Queen Anne period to the superb objects made by Myer Myers, John Heath (worked *ca.* 1760–70), and Daniel Christian Fueter (worked *ca.* 1754–76).

Myers was a Jewish silversmith who made rare ritual silver for old and established congregations in Newport and Philadelphia. He also watched the changing fashions in domestic silver assiduously, and kept rigorously up-to-date in styles as well as in forms rarely made in America (such as candlesticks and cake baskets). Among the masterpieces of this period are at least two objects by Myers, both pierced with fanciful Rococo scrolls—piercing gives visual lightness and grace, which are so necessary a part of the spirit of the Rococo, while the scrolls contribute a rich elegance. It is notable that piercing of this type is a primary regional characteristic of New York silver in this period.

Myers made one of the few known American cake baskets in the 1760's *(Fig. 132)*. Virtually identical to contemporary English examples, the shallow oval bowl is set on a splayed footring, with a long oval bail handle hinged to the rim of the bowl. This simple form is enlivened by complex pierced decoration; regular on the footring, with a series of quatrefoils within flowing geometrical forms, and elaborate on the body, where it is divided into panels. At each end and each side there is a panel of graceful arabesques, separated by panels of intricate repeated quatrefoil designs. The handle has simple crisscross openwork. The edges of the handle, footring, and body (where it is scalloped) are enriched with the small-scale gadrooning characteristic of this period. In harmonizing the different types of pierced decoration and unifying such intricate ornament, Myers created here an elegant and vital Rococo masterpiece.

An even rarer form is the pierced dish-ring by Myers *(Fig. 133)*. Made to support porcelain bowls of hot punch above the rich mahogany surfaces of the period, this form is common in England but rare in America. It is another indication of Myers's attention to fashion. The simple, concave reel-shape is invested with bands of rich, pierced arabesques; the center band may be seen as a series of infinite variations on the letters S and C (Samuel and Susanna Cornell were the original owners of this and other pieces of Myers silver; their initials are on the heart-shaped plaque). Elegant, airy, and fanciful, the plain shape is transformed into a Rococo masterpiece by virtue of its superior decoration.

Daniel Christian Fueter immigrated to New York from Switzerland and brought with him a skilled "chaiser," who may have executed the enchanting Rococo decoration on this gold child's whistle, coral, and bells *(Fig. 134)*. The kind of bauble that appealed to Rococo taste (though not without its practical aspects, since the coral helped the child in teething), this little object is enriched with superb decoration of shells, scrolls, flowers, and a Cupid. That it is of gold—even more

133

134

133. Dish-ring, *ca.* 1760–70, by Myer Myers; H. 4⅝ inches. Yale University Art Gallery, New Haven, Connecticut. The Mabel Brady Garvan Collection.

134. Gold whistle, coral, and bells, *ca.* 1760–70, by Daniel Christian Fueter; L. 5⅜ inches. Yale University Art Gallery, New Haven, Connecticut. The Mabel Brady Garvan Collection.

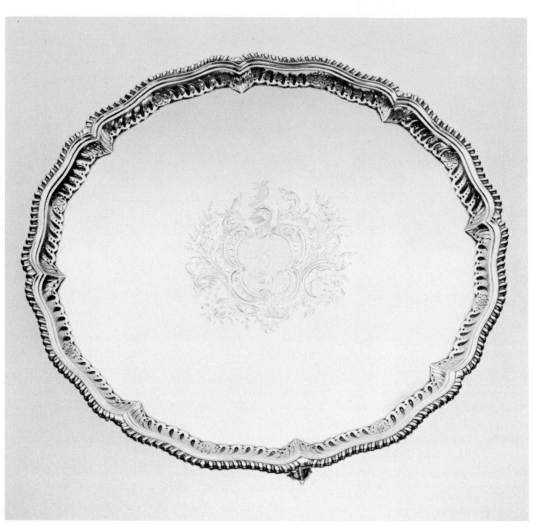

135

135. Salver, *ca.* 1760–70, by John Heath; D.
15⅛ inches. Courtesy of The Henry Francis du
Pont Winterthur Museum, Winterthur, Delaware.

precious than silver—is fully in keeping with its character. Intricate, whimsical, delicate, and beautifully made, it epitomizes the Rococo spirit.

In appearance somewhat plainer, although equally superbly proportioned, is the outstanding salver by John Heath in the Winterthur Museum *(Fig. 135)*. Compared to salvers from the earlier period, *(see Fig. 122)*, this example reveals its stylistic provenance by its elaborately worked rim, essentially composed of sinuous Rococo curves, with a gadrooned outer edge and a "fluted" and engraved inner edge. It stands on three ball-and-claw feet. Its crowning decoration is the engraved cartouche surrounding the Schuyler arms, so beautifully proportioned to the surrounding space, so delicately drawn, and so masterfully executed.

The finest Boston silversmiths working with fully developed Rococo styles were Benjamin Burt (1729–1805) and Paul Revere. Burt was a huge man (tradition has it that he weighed almost four hundred pounds), but his best work is characterized by a delicacy of touch and a marvelous grace. The sauceboat he made for Nathan and Rebecca Pierce of Boston *(Fig. 136)* is one of the most exuberant of all New England Rococo objects. The wonderful uplift and swoop of the heavily beaded rim of the body, the poise and balance of the handle, the elevation and sense of movement that the scroll legs give the piece (with shell knees repeating the shell feet) are all thoroughly imbued with Rococo grace. The chased beading used here is rare on Boston silver; it is more frequently encountered in New York and Philadelphia, where, however, it was generally cast and considerably smaller in scale than Burt's splendid example.

Benjamin Burt's unusual teapot at Yale also possesses extraordinarily graceful qualities *(Fig. 137)*. Were it any higher, it would seem ungainly; but the height of the foot and the unusual proportions of the belly are all part of the Rococo qualities of asymmetry, fragility, and delicate elegance. The harp-type handle was infrequently used at this time, but prefigures the classical type of handle utilized in the ensuing period (the engraved swags are also classical in feeling).

Compared to Burt's work in this period, Revere's is characterized by stronger decoration and a more subdued linear grace. His finest work was undoubtedly executed after the Revolution, yet his Rococo silver has the restraint and implicit quality generally found in masterpieces from the New England region. Revere's teapot made for the Orne family *(Fig. 138)* is one of several in this style that have survived. Its profile is much more tightly compressed than the Burt example, while its decoration is richer—the gadrooning on the foot, the engraved band around the cover, and the details of the cartouche produce an elaborate effect. Revere occasionally chased ornament on teapots as he did on the fine cream jug and sugar bowl he made for the Chandler family in 1761 *(Fig. 139)*. The naturalistic chasing here is more linear than the kind typical of Philadelphia *(see Figs. 128 and 129)*; yet the effect on such small objects is one of robust richness.

Reserve, control, and fastidiousness are the main qualities of Revere's tankard made for the Greene family in 1762 *(Fig. 140)*. Its slender proportions, its "flame" finial, and its cast satyr's mask at the terminal proclaim its Rococo origin. Revere's ability with the graver, or burin, and his use of it for making prints and bookplates are well known; his use of it to execute the arms and cartouche on the tankard *(Fig. 141)* is no less accomplished. The tankard superbly exemplifies the restrained Rococo mode that flourished in this New England center.

Fully developed Rococo tea sets appeared in greater quantity than in the

135

136

Queen Anne period, and, of course, more have survived. Most of the examples from the three cities were fashioned in the prevailing inverted pyriform style, and they appeared in both plain and elaborate versions. Two of the finest Rococo Boston teapots, and a sugar bowl, have already been illustrated *(see Figs. 137, 138, and 139)*; the third indispensable item in the tea set was the cream jug. This took either the regular or the inverted pear-shape, set either on a splayed foot or on three cabriole legs (generally with a shell motif at the juncture, and a trifid-shaped foot). Samuel Casey of Rhode Island *(ca. 1724-ca. 1780)* made an unusual version of the New England cream jug *(Fig. 142)*; the

elaborate, well-designed handle is of double-scroll form, while the feet are the ball-and-claw type common on furniture of this period. The subtle chasing flows loosely in an asymmetrical pattern around the body of the piece.

Peter de Riemer's (1738–1814) well-known tea set highlights all the virtues of the New York Rococo style *(Fig. 143)*. An inverted pyriform body set on a splayed foot is used for the teapot, sugar bowl, and cream jug. Each piece is chased with a bold, rather open naturalistic pattern interspersed with scrolls, producing an undeniably rich, sophisticated effect. The handle of the cream jug is a handsome variant of the double scroll, and the lip is

137

enriched with the Rococo version of gadrooning, a motif repeated on the handle of the cover of the sugar bowl—a regional characteristic of New York silver. The cream jug is further ornamented with decoration on the foot.

A diminutive Rococo teapot by Edmund Milne (worked *ca*. 1757–1813) is an un-

common plain version of this form from Philadelphia *(Fig. 144)*. The band of gadrooning on the foot has been seen on tea-table items from the other cities. By contrast, a cream jug in the Philadelphia Museum by Philip Hulbeart (worked *ca*. 1750–64) is extremely lavish *(Fig. 145)*. The open, shallow chasing reminds one of the Syng coffeepot *(see Fig. 129)*; here, extra flourishes of decoration are added on the handle and on the legs. Philadelphia silversmiths' concern for line and proportion is well illustrated by a tall, handsome sugar bowl *(Fig. 146)* by Joseph and Nathaniel Richardson; the beaded decoration and the galleried rim of the bowl, inside which the cover fits, are both local

136. Sauceboat, *ca.* 1760–70, by Benjamin Burt; H. 5⅜ inches. Yale University Art Gallery, New Haven, Connecticut. The Mabel Brady Garvan Collection.

137. Teapot, *ca.* 1765, by Benjamin Burt; H. 7⅜ inches. Yale University Art Gallery, New Haven, Connecticut. The Mabel Brady Garvan Collection.

138

139

138. Teapot, 1773, by Paul Revere; H. 6⅜
inches. Worcester Art Museum, Worcester, Massachusetts. Gift of Richard K. Thorndike.

139. Sugar bowl and cream jug, 1761, by
Paul Revere; H. (sugar bowl) 6¾ inches. Cour-
tesy of Museum of Fine Arts, Boston. Bequest of
Mrs. Pauline Revere Thayer.

140. Tankard, 1762, by Paul Revere; H. 8⅝ inches. Yale University Art Gallery, New Haven, Connecticut. The Mabel Brady Garvan Collection.

141. Greene arms. Detail of Fig. 140.

142. Cream jug, *ca.* 1760–70, by Samuel Casey; H. 4 inches. Courtesy of Museum of Fine Arts, Boston. Gift of Mrs. Charles Gaston Smith's group.

141

142

143

144

143. Tea set, *ca.* 1765–75, by Pieter de Riemer; H. (teapot) 6¾ inches. Museum of the City of New York. Gift of Mrs. Francis P. Garvan.

144. Teapot, *ca.* 1765–75, by Edmund Milne; H. 5 inches. Courtesy of The Detroit Institute of Arts. The Gibbs-Williams Fund.

145. Cream jug, *ca.* 1750–65, by Philip Hulbeart; H. 4¼ inches. Philadelphia Museum of Art. Given by Walter M. Jeffords (Acc. no. 58-115-1).

146. Sugar bowl, *ca.* 1780–90, by Joseph Richardson, Jr. and Nathaniel Richardson; H. 7¾ inches. Philadelphia Museum of Art. Purchased: Harrison Fund (Acc. no. 55-90-1a, b).

147. Pitcher, *ca.* 1750–60, by Myer Myers; H. 10 inches. Owned by The Henry Ford Museum, Dearborn, Michigan.

145

146

147

148

characteristics. Although considerably larger than other jugs shown here, the bold and beautiful example by Myer Myers *(Fig. 147)* shows how the best silversmiths of this period could adapt the vocabulary of Rococo forms to large objects and still maintain an excellent control of proportion and decoration.

All Rococo coffeepots made in the three cities are variants of the three superb objects we have already seen *(see Figs. 129, 130, and 131)*. An unusually fine example *(Fig. 148)* made by Revere in 1773 shows his characteristic kind of gadrooning (on the foot and the edge of the cover). The handle junctures are rich, thus balancing the elaborate detail of the spout, and the Rococo cartouche is engraved with Revere's customary command. The whole has a cohesiveness and fine sense of proportion rarely found in his work of this period. A year earlier, Revere had made a very

similar coffeepot for the Derby family of Salem, Massachusetts, not set on a splayed foot, however, but rather on three cabriole legs with shell knees and feet—similar to those on the Burt sauceboat *(see Fig. 136)*. In contrast to this Boston piece is a fine and complex example *(Fig. 149)* by the provincial Pennsylvania silversmith Charles Hall, of Lancaster (1742–83). Robust in form and decorated with vigorous chasing of a rather open type on the belly and lip of the body, and on the cover, it epitomizes the best kind of provincial silver in the colonies.

Typical of Boston tankards in the Rococo style is the fine example by Revere at Yale already discussed *(see Fig. 140)*. These objects have relatively slender bodies with the (generally) low midband that first appeared in the second quarter of the century. The baseband, the domed cover with turned-down flange, and the

149

150

151

148. Coffeepot, 1773, by Paul Revere; H. 13½ inches. Worcester Art Museum, Worcester, Massachusetts. Gift of Francis T. and Eliza Sturgis Paine in memory of Frederick William Paine.

149. Coffeepot, *ca.* 1765–75, by Charles Hall; H. 10¾ inches. Owned by The Henry Ford Museum, Dearborn, Michigan.

150. Tankard, *ca.* 1750–60, by Bartholomew Le Roux II; H. 7⅝ inches. Museum of the City of New York. Gift of the Estate of Emily M. Bussing.

151. Tankard, *ca.* 1765–75, by Samuel Tingley; H. 9⅛ inches. Courtesy of The New-York Historical Society, New York City.

long, slender handle we have also seen before. Characteristic of this period, however, is the attractive flame-type finial. Revere's use of a satyr's mask on the handle terminal was idiosyncratic, for most Boston makers preferred the plain, slightly domed kind. A disk applied to the body at the lower handle juncture was also frequently used in this period.

New York makers still preferred flat-topped tankards but distinguished themselves from their Boston colleagues by utilizing a double-scroll handle and occasionally an openwork thumbpiece *(Fig. 150).* The form of double-scroll handle used on this fine example by Bartholomew Le Roux II (worked *ca.* 1738–63) is characteristic of New York, with the terminal in the form of an extra flourish. The baseband is also typically elaborate. Midbands seldom appear on tankards made in this city in the third quarter of the century.

Samuel Tingley of New York (worked *ca.* 1767–96) made an unusual pear-shaped tankard for the Van Rensselaer family *(Fig. 151),* which is close to contemporary Philadelphia examples in form. The domed cover and openwork thumbpiece were frequently used in that city *(see Fig. 152).* Yet the engraved cartouche has an elaboration and commanding size we have seen frequently on New York silver of all periods. Many Philadelphia tankards were pyriform in this period, with a double-scroll handle. An example by the fine maker Richard Humphreys (worked *ca.* 1771–96), illustrated here *(Fig. 152),* has a higher splayed foot, a higher domed cover, and a more elaborate openwork thumbpiece (typical of Philadelphia) than comparable New York pieces *(see Fig. 151).* The double-scroll handle—typical of Philadelphia but different from that of New York—with the flat central join and the flat, shield-shaped terminal should also be noted. Straight-sided Philadelphia tankards with a simi-

larly domed cover and single-scroll handle were not unknown at this time.

Boston and New York canns also vary slightly in the fully developed Rococo period. Both kinds are generally pear-shaped, with a splayed foot and a double-scroll handle ending in a solid, scrolled terminal; however, the Boston cann often has a molded strut with a scrolled juncture at the upper joining of handle and body *(Fig. 153),* while the New York form frequently has an inverted shell-shaped juncture *(Fig 154).* (The beautifully pro-

152

153

152. Tankard, *ca.* 1770–75, by Richard Humphreys; H. 8¾ inches. Collection of Mrs. Edsel B. Ford, Grosse Pointe Shores, Michigan.

153. Cann, *ca.* 1760–70, by Benjamin Burt; H. 5¾ inches. Yale University Art Gallery, New Haven, Connecticut. The Mabel Brady Garvan Collection.

154. Covered cann, *ca.* 1760–70, by Myer Myers; H. 6⅝ inches. Yale University Art Gallery, New Haven, Connecticut. The Mabel Brady Garvan Collection.

154

155

156

portioned example by Myers illustrated here is rare in its utilization of a separate cover.) Philadelphia canns are usually similar to Boston examples in form and detail.

Compared to the magnificent examples of the form from the preceding periods, two-handled cups of the third quarter of the eighteenth century are undistinguished. No fine examples from Boston or Philadelphia have survived, and only a very few from New York. The largest and best known is that by Elias Pelletreau (1726–1810), engraved with the Van Cortlandt arms in an earlier style cartouche *(Fig. 155)*. Aesthetically, it is an imbalanced object, for the foot is overpowered by the gradually flaring body and by the large, high-domed cover surmounted by an ungainly finial. Furthermore, the placement of the midband squashes the arms into an inferior position on the body. The grooved, double-scroll handles, with long struts at the junctures, are in typical Rococo style.

Indubitably the most famous American silver bowl, celebrated for its historic associations rather than its formal qualities (which are modest) is the "Sons of Liberty" punch bowl made by Paul Revere in 1768 *(Fig. 156)*. It commemorates the vote of the Massachusetts House of Representatives not to rescind a letter sent to other colonies urging resistance to repressive measures, and symbolizes the growing resistance of many colonists to highhanded policies from London. The inevitable symbols of liberty cap, Magna Carta,

Bill of Rights, and John Wilkes (the English political reformer and agitator) are all invoked in the engraved decoration.

Aesthetically more successful is the bowl made by John Heath for the Van Cortlandt family and engraved with their arms and crest in a flowing Rococo cartouche *(Fig. 157)*. Almost as wide but shallower than the Revere example, it is more nearly hemispherical, with a wide splayed foot well proportioned to the size of the body.

Although plain bowls are not uncommon in this period, examples bearing chased decoration, such as the fine piece by Richard, son of Peter van Dyck (1717–70), are rare *(Fig. 158)*. The chasing is fine and subtle, and so shallow as to be closer to engraving than the normal type of Rococo *repoussé*. Another New York bowl illustrated here, by Myer Myers, is notable for the richness of its chasing *(Fig. 159)*. It closely resembles the bowl from the De Riemer tea set made in the same city *(see Fig. 143)*, although it is considerably larger than the normal sugar bowl.

No list of bowls in this period would be complete without mention of the third known Monteith from New England, made by Daniel Henchman (1730–75) for the president of Dartmouth College in 1771. Approximately the same size as the Heath bowl but higher and with a leaner look, the Henchman bowl has a simple scrolled molding at the rim.

Mention should be made of strainers, which appear in some quantity in this period. They were used in the preparation of punch served from bowls such as those just discussed, or on the tea table. The necessity of piercing the bowl afforded the imaginative silversmith an opportunity to create attractive patterns (as he also did on the covers of casters and on the sides of chafing dishes). The scroll handles, long enough to support the strainer on top of the bowl, could also be

157

158

decorated with graceful arabesques. Perhaps the finest such object from this period is the well-known strainer made by the Rhode Island silversmith, Jonathan Clarke (*ca.* 1705–70) for Jabez Bowen of Providence in 1765 *(Fig. 160)*. The apposite notation is formed of tiny perforations surrounding the intricate floral pattern in the center of the bowl.

Small supports, or "dish-crosses," to hold bowls and heat their contents, also appeared occasionally in the Rococo period,

mainly in New York. Consisting of two square strips hinged around a spirit lamp in the center, with legs (and bracket supports above) sliding on the strips to accommodate different sized bowls, these are elegant and unusual objects.

Condiment sets, which have survived only occasionally from the Queen Anne period, are more common in the fully developed Rococo style. A few cruet sets in the most elegant English fashion are also known; these combine sugar, salt, and pepper casters (pepper boxes are rare by this time), and similarly shaped casters for mustard and vinegar. One such cruet stand was made by Daniel Christian Fueter of New York for an elaborate set of English casters, which are dated 1752 *(Fig. 161)*. Fueter's decoration is perfectly in accord with the casters, although it is limited to shell feet, elegant scroll handle, and a cast Rococo cartouche. A few mustard pots, small and cylindrical, with or without a glass liner, and occasionally

---

157. Bowl, *ca.* 1760, by John Heath; D. 10⅛ inches. Yale University Art Gallery, New Haven, Connecticut. The John Marshall Phillips Collection.

158. Bowl, *ca.* 1745–60, by Richard van Dyck; D. 7⅜ inches. Yale University Art Gallery, New Haven, Connecticut. The Mabel Brady Garvan Collection.

159. Bowl, *ca.* 1750–60, by Myer Myers; D. 6 inches. Courtesy of The Detroit Institute of Arts. Gibbs-Williams Fund and by exchange.

159

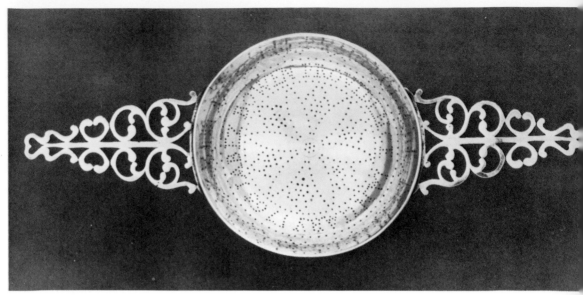

160

161

152

162

160. Strainer, 1765, by Jonathan Clarke; L. 11⅞ inches. Yale University Art Gallery, New Haven, Connecticut. The Mabel Brady Garvan Collection.

161. Cruet stand, *ca.* 1760–70, by Daniel Christian Fueter; H. 9⅟₁₆ inches. The Heritage Foundation, Old Deerfield, Massachusetts.

162. Pair of coasters, *ca.* 1750–70, by Myer Myers; D. 4⅞ inches. Courtesy of The New-York Historical Society, New York City.

163. Snuff box, *ca.* 1750–70, by Joseph Richardson; L. 3⅟₁₆ inches. Yale University Art Gallery, New Haven, Connecticut. The Mabel Brady Garvan Collection.

rim, and a beaded band at the base. Again, the large number of imported coasters accounts for the scarcity of American-made ones—many American silversmiths at this time advertised imported sets for sale in their own shops.

Small boxes, ever popular with men for tobacco and snuff and with women for patches (among other things), were made in the three cities in both gold and silver in this period. One handsome example by Joseph Richardson *(Fig. 163)* reveals the

pierced in attractive patterns, have survived; but the majority of condiment sets are either baluster-shaped (as in the preceding period) or similarly shaped but with the Rococo, inverted pear-shaped body.

In the same vein as the above are coasters, only a few of which are known. A delightful and rare pair was made by Myer Myers for the Schuyler family *(Fig. 162).* They are pierced in Myers's familiar fashion, with an undulating, gadrooned

163

164

165

intrinsic richness that these small objects could achieve when elaborately chased. They were more frequently engraved, however; examples by Revere, Myers, and other leading silversmiths are known.

An elegant example of the Rococo chafing dish *(Fig. 164)* is the piece probably made for the first president of Columbia University, William Johnson, by the Connecticut maker Robert Fairchild (1703–94). Slight differences exist between this and the earlier Boston example by Jacob Hurd *(see Fig. 116)*. Fairchild utilized the familiar elements of widely scrolled legs and scroll feet to great effect, giving the object a distinctive flair. Few other such elegant pieces by silversmiths of this period are known.

Benjamin Burt's superb sauceboat *(see Fig. 136)* stands apart from the majority of contemporary New England examples by its great verve; the heavily beaded rather than serrated rim is also unusual. Paul Revere made sauceboats with shell knees and feet and serrated rim, but he is better remembered for the delightful

166

---

small pair derived from porcelain prototypes *(Fig. 165).* The apparent casualness of the gadrooned decoration on the splayed footring and on the rim in no way belies the intrinsically delightful quality of these small objects. An even richer variant was made in Philadelphia by Richard Humphreys, who is also noted for the silver he made for General Washington's use in the field. This exquisite object *(Fig. 166)* has great delicacy and finesse of detail, with much of the Rococo grace of Burt's example. The shape of the foot and the elevation and detail of the handle are particularly notable, giving the object a sophistication associated with the best Philadelphia artistry of this time.

The salver form afforded the silversmith an excellent opportunity to contrast large plain areas with highly elaborate borders; the face of the salver also called for virtuoso displays of engraving. The outstanding example by John Heath *(see Fig. 135)* has already revealed the exquisite form and decoration that is typical of this kind of piece in the Rococo period. Almost identical in outline is the huge salver *(Fig. 167)* by Lewis Fueter (worked *ca.* 1770–80), the son of Daniel Christian Fueter. One of the earliest of the important New York presentation pieces, which will appear more frequently in the subsequent chapters, this salver was given to Captain Sowers by Governor Tryon and the General Assembly of New York in 1773. It is engraved with the arms of New York and assorted military emblems within a massive foliate wreath. In its florid appearance and great size, it is at the other end of the Rococo scale from the

155

167

168

delicate, pierced masterpieces by Myer Myers.

Daniel Christian Fueter also made large salvers; one of these has an outline of considerable beauty *(Fig. 168)*. The curve and reverse-curve of the gadrooned rim effectively contrasts with the plain face of the salver. Smaller than the New York arms on the previous example, the cartouche surrounding the Provoost arms here reveals, in its delicacy and control, the hand of a master.

Engraved cartouches on Boston and New York silver were rarely alike in either the Queen Anne or the fully developed Rococo periods. Fueter's example should be compared with Revere's surrounding the Chandler arms *(Fig. 169)*; both are distinguished by great subtlety and finesse, although the New York example is more freely flowing and less tightly compressed. The Revere salver has a characteristically Rococo outline, with a bold rim of intricate rhythms and scrolls as extra flourishes. This kind of border appears on silver of all the major cities at this time.

167. Salver, 1773, by Lewis Fueter; D. 21¾ inches. Courtesy of The New-York Historical Society, New York City.

168. Salver, *ca.* 1750–75, by Daniel Christian Fueter; D. 15⅝ inches. The Metropolitan Museum of Art, New York. Bequest of Charles Allen Munn, 1924.

169. Salver, *ca.* 1761, by Paul Revere; D. 13⅛ inches. Courtesy of Museum of Fine Arts, Boston.

169

Fine Rococo candlesticks are even rarer than the Queen Anne examples. Only a few pairs are known; of these, the pair made by Myers for the Livingston family with accompanying snuffers and stand is the finest *(Fig. 170)*. Tall and delicate in profile, intricate in their scroll decoration, they give the appearance of being at once rich and fragile. The stem is a Rococo variant of the baluster stem we have previously seen. Obviously patterned after contemporary English examples, they may even have been cast from a mold taken from an actual English piece (a similar pair bearing Myers's mark also bears the easily discernible traces of English marks). The snuffers and stand *(Fig. 171)* are also embellished with shell and scroll decoration.

Spoons made in this period are similar to those of the Queen Anne style, except that the rattail on the front of the handle is greatly shortened so that it becomes little more than a V. Often there is a shell on the back of the bowl at the handle juncture. Toward the end of the period,

157

170

the handle-end becomes downward bent and frequently decorated with bright-cutting (see p. 163). Occasionally, on the larger spoons and ladles, the bowl is fluted; an exceptional example (Fig. 172) by Daniel Van Voorhis of New York (1751–1824) has a chased foliate design between the flutes at the edge of the bowl. Also typical of the exquisite detail so often found in Rococo silver is a small shoe buckle by Joseph Richardson (Fig. 173). Porringers of this period retain the traditional "keyhole" handle design (see Fig. 127).

171

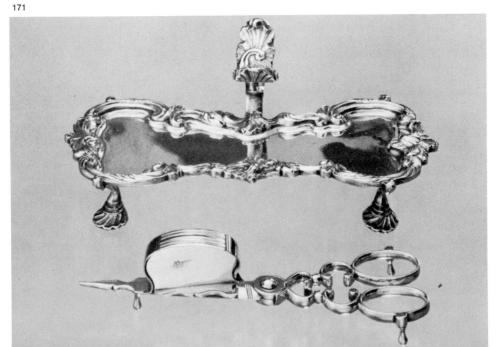

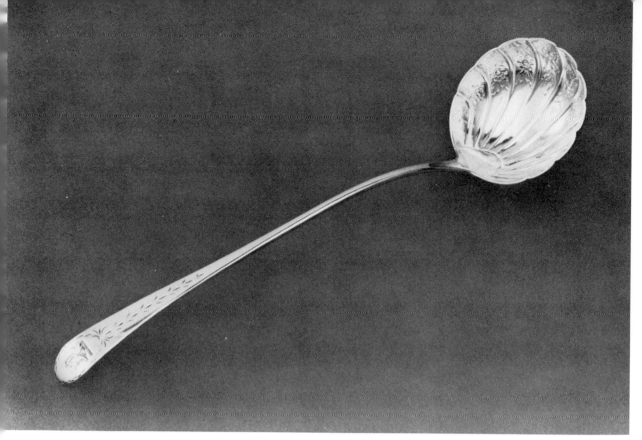

172

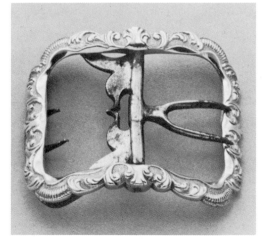

170. Candlestick, *ca.* 1755–70, by Myer Myers; H. 10⅛ inches. Yale University Art Gallery, New Haven, Connecticut. The Mabel Brady Garvan Collection.

171. Snuffers and stand, *ca.* 1755–70, by Myer Myers; L. (snuffers) 7⅜ inches. Yale University Art Gallery, New Haven, Connecticut. The Mabel Brady Garvan Collection.

172. Ladle, *ca.* 1780–90, by Daniel van Voorhis; L. 15⅝ inches. Yale University Art Gallery, New Haven, Connecticut. The Mabel Brady Garvan Collection.

173. Gold shoe buckle, *ca.* 1740–50, by Joseph Richardson; L. 1⅞ inches. Yale University Art Gallery, New Haven, Connecticut. The Mabel Brady Garvan Collection.

CHAPTER SIX

The Classical Taste
of the
Early Republic

From the cataclysm of the Revolution, America emerged victorious but also rather precarious, politically and economically. Some years elapsed before the cities were able to recuperate from war damage, as well as from the loss of a significantly wealthy part of society—the Loyalists, about thirty thousand of whom left New York alone in 1783. The situation was greatly aggravated by reprisals from England in the form of world-trade restrictions. Because of the political disquietude in America in the years following the war, as well as the economic plight, the 1780's were not particularly profitable years for high-quality craftsmen. Indeed, it was not until about fifteen years after

174. Tea urn, 1774, by Richard Humphreys; H. 21½ inches. Private collection. Photograph courtesy of Philadelphia Museum of Art. Photograph by A. J. Wyatt, Staff Photographer.

175. Tea urn, 1800, by Paul Revere; H. 18¹⁵⁄₁₆ inches. Courtesy Massachusetts Historical Society, Boston. Photograph courtesy of Museum of Fine Arts, Boston.

174

175

the start of the Revolutionary War that most silversmiths resumed significant production. Paul Revere's finest work, for example, was done in the last decade of the eighteenth century.

By the early 1790's, however, England's involvement in the French Revolutionary Wars meant that she was less able to maintain and supervise trade restrictions, and, as both England and France stood in need of supplies from America and profited by the use of American shipping, the American economy began to improve rapidly. Now it was New York that expanded more vigorously than Boston or Philadelphia; by 1797, trade in that port was six times greater than in 1792, and had exceeded that of Philadelphia. And the volume doubled again in the next decade. Except for a recession at the time of the War of 1812, this state of affairs continued until the end of the nineteenth century.

At the turn of the century, New York (with sixty thousand inhabitants) was almost as large as Philadelphia (with seventy thousand), which in turn was virtually three times the size of Boston (now smaller than Baltimore). Accomplished architects were at work in each of the cities designing and supervising the erection of lovely classical buildings, both private and public: Pierre Charles L'Enfant in New York, Benjamin Latrobe in Philadelphia, and Charles Bulfinch in Boston. Charles Willson Peale continued to refine and improve upon his pictorial abilities, while he and his prolific family, and the often-brilliant Gilbert Stuart (first in Philadelphia and later in Boston) immortalized the countenances of the founding fathers of the Republic in appropriate classical manner. Duncan Phyfe and Thomas Seymour made much elegant furniture in the latest Sheraton and Hepplewhite styles. A substantial number of silversmiths of excellent quality worked in both the larger cities; by the turn of the

century, more than thirty silversmiths advertised regularly in the Philadelphia newspapers. Through an increasingly sophisticated technology, rolled sheets of silver became widely available, and undoubtedly contributed a smoothness and lightness to the craftsmen's work. Yet society demanded the same aesthetic of the silversmith as it did of the cabinetmaker—elegant forms with plentiful use of geometric motifs, light weight, and taut, smooth surfaces.

The ways of the old, esteemed republics of Greece and Rome, increasingly brought to light by archaeology, undoubtedly appealed to the citizens of the newly formed American republic as paradigms. Laws, customs, forms—all the qualities symbolic of the old virtue would adorn and hopefully ennoble the new. The early classical period in America really started with the new Republic and ended with the first major external threat against it—the War of 1812; the period thus falls conveniently between the two wars with England. Yet it cannot be denied that the influence of English taste, which had displayed a preference for identical classical forms and ornaments since the 1760's, was as predominant in this period as it had been before.

The earliest classical silver object created in America was actually made two years before the Revolution. This important object is a tea urn by Richard Humphreys of Philadelphia (*Fig. 174*), which was given by members of the first Constitutional Congress to its secretary, Charles Thomson, in 1774. While this piece, which is extremely English in character, displays all the qualities of the classical period, the inscription that dates it to this early year (one would otherwise think the object was made in the 1790's) is in typical Rococo lettering within a superb Rococo cartouche. It was engraved by James Smither of Philadelphia, a professional engraver, and is so signed. The object is urn-shaped

—the basic form of the classical period, meant to symbolize the purity, restraint, and virtue of the republican ideal. Complementing this form is a series of geometric shapes, such as the square, rectangle, circle, and oval, all of which are utilized in the decorative vocabulary of the classical period. In cross-section, the urn is circular, a shape emphasized by various bands of applied ornament, such as the simulated galleried (or arcaded) rim of the body and the bands of beading on cover and foot. Instead of the graceful scroll-shaped handles to which we have become accustomed, there are small, squared handles, by no means successfully integrated into the proportions of the object. The high splayed foot is set on a square base, decorated with the same kind of ornament as on the rim of the body, which is then set on four ball feet; this motif became more popular around the turn of the century. Finally, there is a broad band of acanthus leaves at the bottom of the body, articulating the large expanse of otherwise plain surface.

It is valuable to compare this piece with a Boston tea urn made by Paul Revere more than a quarter of a century later *(Fig. 175)*. The Boston urn was presented to Captain Gamaliel Bradford in 1800. Unusually slender in proportion, compared to most urn forms from this city, it stands on a square base with four ball-and-claw feet. The handles are scrolled and are tall and slender in the manner of cream jugs of the classical period. The tall cover adds perfect poise and elegance to the object, while the whole is decorated with applied, reeded moldings typical of Boston, and bright-cut borders in a style that also marks the northern origin of this piece. (Bright-cutting was widely used in this period; it differs from engraving in that it is not simply a continuous line of varying width, but a succession of small gouges made at an oblique angle. These give a shimmering effect to the design that complements the very smooth surfaces surrounding it.) One of the earliest uses of it appears on an inverted pear-shaped teapot by Benjamin Burt *[see Fig. 137]* decorated with classical swags and dated 1765.) While not so tall or so important an object as the Humphreys urn, the Revere piece is more cohesive and more perfectly proportioned.

How the urn-form was adapted to the all-important objects for the tea table—especially in vogue in this period—is splendidly shown by a tea set *(Fig. 176)* by Abraham Dubois of Philadelphia (worked *ca.* 1777–1807). Made about twenty years later than the Humphreys urn, the tea set is a model of refined outline and lovely proportions. The teapot is set diagonally on a square base, which is slimmer and more sucessfully integrated than the base of the tea urn, while the cover shows the development to a graduated shoulder (which helps to break up the large areas of plain body) that is only hinted at in the Humphreys urn. Slim bands of beading accentuate various points on the pot and on the top and bottom of the spout, and articulate the plain areas, while the urn-shaped finial is the appropriate climax of the piece. The scroll on the wooden handle is a pleasing variation. On the beautiful sugar urn one can see the full effect of the previously mentioned galleried rim, so typical a Philadelphia characteristic in this period. It marks the transition between the body and the long, elegantly designed cover. The cream jug is unusual in having a cover—only a few of these were made in Philadelphia and New York in this period. The slender outline of the handle perfectly conveys the smaller scale of this piece. Totally devoid of engraving, this tea set relies for its appeal on profile, proportion, and surface—here, in keeping with its restraint and purity, as perfectly smooth and polished as possible.

The epitome of the classical tea and

176

coffee service is surely that by Joseph Richardson, Jr. (1752–1831), of Philadelphia *(Fig. 177)*. Oval in cross-section and utilizing the later variant of the urn-form, with broad, graduated flutes, the service is a *tour de force* of elegance. The silversmith cleverly varied the repeated ovals of the base, body, grooved spout, and finial, and also the strap-handles of the cream jugs. The covers and handles on the two larger pots are also successfully varied. The graduated shoulder is used with great

effect on the larger of the two pots, which also achieves a more sucessful synthesis of vertical and horizontal accents—at the foot, shoulder, cover, and dome. Simply decorated with the owner's initials, this service is further distinguished by virtue of its being one of the most complete from this period still in existence.

Classical silver made in New York is outstanding. Numerous tea and coffee services are distinguished by elegant proportions and superlative detail. A rela-

177

176. Tea set, *ca.* 1785–95, by Abraham Dubois; H. (teapot) 11⅜ inches. Yale University Art Gallery, New Haven, Connecticut. The Mabel Brady Garvan Collection.

177. Tea and coffee set, *ca.* 1790–1800, by Joseph Richardson, Jr.; H. (coffeepot) 14¼ inches. Philadelphia Museum of Art. Given by Gordon A. Hardwick in memory of Marjory Taylor Hardwick (Acc. no. 62-228-1,2,3,4; 63-4-1,2,3).

tively large number of makers maintained a high degree of quality in their work. One of the best known of these (through his associations with George Washington and his making of money, including the famous doubloons) is Ephraim Brasher (1744–1810). The teapot and sugar urn he made for Marinus Willett *(Fig. 178)* reveal the highest qualities of design and execution. The teapot is oval, with a high collar and domed cover and fine beading at the junctures. The double-scroll handle enhances the elegance of the piece. Typical of New York are the bright-cut bands at top and base of the body, and the delicate foliate shield within elaborate swags on the side. These bright-cut motifs—together with the collar and urn-finial—are repeated on the exceptionally fine sugar urn. Tall, erect, and of outstanding proportions, this object surely epitomizes the formal excellence that the best silver of this period could achieve.

An unusual and highly ornate sugar urn of boat shape illustrates a different facet of the New York style *(Fig. 179)*. Made for the De Peyster family by Daniel van Voorhis and Gerrit Schank (working in partnership 1791–92), the octagonal urn is enriched with scalloped and bright-cut vertical bands on the foot, at the lip of the body, and below the dome of the cover. Bright-cutting in the form of border designs, dotted lines, swags, and pendent medallions emphasizes the paneled shape of the piece. Surmounting the whole is a pineapple finial with rayed leaves at the base, so typical of New York. Its very decorative richness gives an extra dimension to this well-proportioned object and proves that even in this period, surface elaboration was highly prized by certain elements of the population.

An unusual form in American silver is the large and ambitious cake basket *(Fig. 180)* by Simeon Bayley (worked *ca.* 1789–96). Of superb quality, the boat-shaped body is set on a high splayed foot; it is essentially an elongated octagon. The typical large expanses of smooth surface are varied by the engraved foliate border and the pierced, engraved, and bright-cut edge repeated on the foot. The faceted handle is an appropriate and elegant climax to this choice object, which was made for Edward and Mary (Elsworth) Dunscombe. Their initials can be seen within the bright-cut and engraved cartouche of draped-ermine form, which is also typical of New York in this period.

Boston silversmithing of the early classical period presents a different picture from that of New York or Philadelphia, where there was a multiplicity of excellent talents at work. Paul Revere dominated the scene, though he became increasingly diverted from this craft by his activities with a foundry and, later, a copper mill. His best work in the classical taste, however, is far superior in quality to that of the preceding period, and to that of the relatively few Boston silversmiths who were his contemporaries. One of Revere's finest objects is the superb tray *(Fig. 181)* that he made for Elias Hasket Derby of Salem in 1797. It is imposing in size and execution. Oval in form, with the broad scallops at the rim subtly repeating the shape, it combines the broad expanse of smooth surface popular in this period, with such excellent detail as the small flame or leaf motif capping each scallop. In the middle, an engraved and bright-cut oval wreath (different from the preceding New York cartouche) surrounds the finely designed cipher of the owner's initials. Fixed bail-type handles are applied at each end.

That the outline of this object is a clever variation (or inversion) of the broadly fluted oval shape we have already seen *(see Fig. 177)*, can be illustrated more clearly by comparing it with another superb Revere piece, a classical teapot *(Fig. 182)*. The brilliant, pristine effect of the broad oval flutes repeated boldly

178

178. Teapot and sugar urn, *ca.* 1790–1800, by Ephraim Brasher; H. (urn) 11¼ inches. Museum of the City of New York. Gift of Mrs. William H. Wheelock.

179

around the oval body is exceptional. The tapered spout is also oval in cross-section, and the outline of the handle further repeats the shape. The cover is almost flat, to interfere as little as possible with the outline without terminating the body too sharply at the top. The bright-cut oval swags at the top and bottom of the body enhance the fluted design. In its sophistication and purity of form, it is one of the masterpieces of design in the classical period.

The third Boston masterpiece illustrated here is a rare form in these years. It is one of a set of four two-handled cups by Joseph Loring (1743–1815), made about 1790 for the Brattle Street Church in Boston (*Fig. 183*). The urn-shaped body is simply ornamented, with slight, reeded bands at base, lip, and below the finial, providing horizontal accents, and a simple inscription in appropriate Roman letters in a bright-cut oval frame, hung from a bowknot. The elegant handles emphasize the urn-shape of the body, on a slightly different plane and on a different scale. The cup is proportionately two units wide and three high, exactly the opposite

179. Sugar urn, 1791–92, by Van Voorhis and Schanck; H. 7¼ inches. Museum of the City of New York. Gift of Mrs. De Peyster Hosmer.

180. Cake basket, *ca.* 1790–95, by Simeon Bayley; L. 13⅞ inches. Museum of the City of New York. Gift of George Elsworth Dunscombe.

of the earliest known Boston two-handled covered cup *(see Fig. 6).* Its intricate geometrical forms and proportions and the obvious coherence of the whole form mark this as an outstanding piece.

Classical tea and coffee services mani-fest a greater diversity of shape than those of earlier periods. Teapots in particular were of several kinds—generally ranging from the very pleasing to the beautiful—in contrast to the rather limited range of the inverted pyriform in the preceding period. Revere's most successful creation has already been illustrated *(see Fig. 182);* he also utilized the drum-shaped teapot frequently *(Fig. 184),* as did silversmiths in Philadelphia but rarely in New York. Revere's examples are distinguished by heavy beading (not so small or so fine as that often seen on Philadelphia pieces) at

181

181. Salver, 1797, by Paul Revere; L. 17 inches. Yale University Art Gallery, New Haven, Connecticut. The Mabel Brady Garvan Collection.

182. Teapot, *ca.* 1790–95, by Paul Revere; H. 6 inches. Yale University Art Gallery, New Haven, Connecticut. The Mabel Brady Garvan Collection.

the top and bottom of the slightly tapered body and on the cover. Shoulder and domed cover are finely proportioned, while the shallow fluting of the spout and the handle-sockets is a subtle and pleasing variation. The slender, airy quality of the cipher within pendent fronds is perfectly in accord with the slender elegance of the object.

Philadelphia teapots of this type generally have a broader drum without the bold, concave shoulder of the Boston piece. An example by Joseph and Nathan-

182

iel Richardson at Yale *(Fig. 185)* illustrates the characteristics of that city: the
bold baseband, the gentle, convex shoulder, the rounded, rather fat spout and
handle-sockets. Philadelphia examples are
also known with a galleried rim on the
shoulder around the cover, and with a
well-defined pineapple finial (apparently
a symbol of hospitality), which was also
often used in New York. The survival of
the Philadelphia-style Rococo cartouche
and shoulder decoration on the Richardson piece should also be noticed.

Oval teapots were extremely popular in
this period, and variations on the form
were frequently utilized by New York silversmiths. One such variation was boat-
shaped, with a broad flute on each side
toward the ends, as this late example by
William G. Forbes (1751–1840) shows
(Fig. 186). The narrow footring, the high
cover, and the type and superior quality
of the bright-cut ornament are distinct
New York characteristics.

Another alternative was the rectangular
shape with chamfered corners (or irregu-

184

185

183. Two-handled covered cup, *ca.* 1790, by Joseph Loring; H. 11¾ inches. Yale University Art Gallery, New Haven, Connecticut. The Mabel Brady Garvan Collection.

184. Teapot, *ca.* 1782–85, by Paul Revere; H. 6⅝ inches. Yale University Art Gallery, New Haven, Connecticut. The Mabel Brady Garvan Collection.

185. Teapot, *ca.* 1780–90, by Joseph Richardson, Jr., and Nathaniel Richardson; H. 6¹¹⁄₁₆ inches. Yale University Art Gallery, New Haven, Connecticut. The Mabel Brady Garvan Collection.

173

lar-octagon shape), such as the splendid teapot by Simeon Bayley in the Museum of the City of New York *(Fig. 187)*. Subtly counterbalancing the otherwise rigid geometrical form are the variations of oval cover, spout, and engraved shield, and the flat, urn-shaped finial. A conforming tray on simple curved triangular legs adds further luster to this fine piece. This New York type of cartouche has already been mentioned *(see Fig. 180)*.

Compared to these New York examples, the other type of oval pot created by Revere *(Fig. 188)*, with domed cover, bands of reeding like those on the Loring two-handled cup *(see Fig. 183)*, and bands of bright-cutting (similar in their patterns

186. Teapot, *ca.* 1800–1810, by William G. Forbes; H. 8¾₆ inches. Yale University Art Gallery, New Haven, Connecticut. The Mabel Brady Garvan Collection.

187. Teapot and stand, *ca.* 1785–95, by Simeon Bayley; H. 7 inches. Museum of the City of New York. Gift of George Elsworth Dunscombe.

188. Teapot, *ca.* 1795–1800, by Paul Revere; H. 7¾₆ inches. Yale University Art Gallery, New Haven, Connecticut. The Mabel Brady Garvan Collection.

---

of movement to those on the Forbes teapot), seems somewhat pedestrian.

The final variant of the oval shape illustrated here is a Philadelphia tea or

186

187

coffeepot *(Fig. 189)* by John McMullin (1765–1843). It is the least attractive of this whole selection. The body appears to be out of balance with the foot, spout, and handle (which is squared in the classical manner). In the somewhat bulky aspect of its parts, it prefigures the succeeding Empire period and presumably dates from the end of the first decade of the nineteenth century.

Sugar urns are among the purest and loveliest forms made at this time. Examples from each major city illustrated here reveal regional differences in form and decoration. The Boston example, made in 1799 by Revere for presentation to Edmund Hartt, who built the frigate *Boston* for the American Navy, is typically squat *(Fig. 190);* the cover is insufficiently tall to balance the broad body. (Revere's important gold urn that Martha Washington presented to the Massachusetts Masonic Order in 1800 has similarly ungraceful proportions.) As with the oval teapot *(see Fig. 188),* Revere chose a dense bright-cut design and an undistinguished finial.

The New York example *(Fig. 191)* was made by John Burger (worked *ca.* 1780–1800). It, too, is rather broad in appearance, an effect that the domed cover, typical of New York, does not dispel. The

189. Tea or coffeepot, *ca.* 1800–1810, by John McMullin; H. 8⅞ inches. Yale University Art Gallery, New Haven, Connecticut. The Mabel Brady Garvan Collection.

190. Sugar urn, 1799, by Paul Revere; H. 8⅜ inches. Courtesy of Museum of Fine Arts, Boston. Gift of James Longley.

191. Sugar urn, *ca.* 1790–1800, by John Burger; H. 8⁵⁄₁₆ inches. Yale University Art Gallery, New Haven, Connecticut. The Mabel Brady Garvan Collection.

delicate and shimmering bright-cut decoration is more successful than Revere's. Swags on the body are repeated in lighter form on the cover, while the rayed design on the edge of the cover is repeated on the foot. How delicate is the border at the lip of the body compared to that by Revere!

The Philadelphia urn by John Germon (worked *ca.* 1782–1816) is the slenderest and most elegant of the three *(Fig. 192).* The simplicity of the bright-cut decoration complements the richness of the beaded bands and the galleried rim. The tall cover, crowned by an urn-finial, makes a perfect counterpoise to the body. This selection, however, should not obscure the exceptional elegance of which New York makers were capable in this period. One superb example by Brasher *(see Fig. 178)* has already been shown; another, by William G. Forbes *(Fig. 193),* bears vivid witness to the beauty of the most successful versions of the form.

The final variant illustrated here is an important presentation piece: an urn made about 1800 by Joseph Lownes of Philadelphia for presentation to Captain William Anderson *(Fig. 194).* The heavily engraved and bright-cut border at the lip, the eagle finial, the lion's-mask hasp, and

192

193

192. Sugar urn, *ca.* 1790–1800, by John Germon; H. 10⁷⁄₁₆ inches. Yale University Art Gallery, New Haven, Connecticut. The Mabel Brady Garvan Collection.

193. Sugar urn, *ca.* 1790–1800, by William G. Forbes; H. 10⅛ inches. Yale University Art Gallery, New Haven, Connecticut. The Mabel Brady Garvan Collection.

194. Sugar urn, *ca.* 1800, by Joseph Lownes; H. 18 inches. The Philip Hammerslough Collection. Photograph courtesy of Wadsworth Atheneum, Hartford.

---

the knop on the stem all prefigure the fully classical silver of the Empire period.

Revere made an alternative type of the classical sugar-holder—an attractive fluted oval basket, typically English in style *(Fig. 195)*. This form persisted into the following style period, as the delightfully proportioned example *(Fig. 196)* by the Philadelphian Josiah H. Lownes (worked *ca.* 1820) proves.

Cream jugs for the tea set were generally helmet-shaped (akin to the urn form of the teapot), standing on a high foot, and with a thin strap-handle in a high arch. Variants of this were even closer to the teapot in form, with a high concave neck and occasionally a cover surmounted by a finial *(see Fig. 177)*. An unusual version by Revere was based on a ceramic form then popular, the Liverpool type of creamware jug *(Fig. 197)*. Delicate in scale, with attractive decoration at the base, on the reeded lip, and on the handle, this small jug has further classical decoration on the body.

Tea caddies appear in greater quantity in this period than any other. Generally oval, they are rarely as elaborate as the example by Daniel van Voorhis illustrated here *(Fig. 198)*. Although the typically New York bright-cut decoration might be considered overabundant, there is no

194

179

195

197

196

180

198

195. Sugar basket, *ca.* 1798, by Paul Revere; L. 6³⁄₁₆ inches. Courtesy of Museum of Fine Arts, Boston.

196. Sugar basket, *ca.* 1820, by Josiah H. Lownes; H. 7⅛ inches. Owned by The Henry Ford Museum, Dearborn, Michigan.

197. Cream jug, *ca.* 1800, by Paul Revere; H. 5 inches. Courtesy of Museum of Fine Arts, Boston. Bequest of Mrs. Pauline Revere Thayer.

198. Tea caddy, *ca.* 1800–1810, by Daniel van Voorhis; H. 4½ inches. Courtesy of The New-York Historical Society, New York City.

---

denying its exceptionally fine, pristine quality.

In this period, silversmiths produced a fascinating and diverse range of objects for the tea table, with infinite variations on the basic types. In addition to those already seen three services illustrated here are excellent variants. The Philadelphia set *(Fig. 199)* is composed of objects by three makers. The two pots and the slop bowl are by Samuel Williamson (worked *ca.* 1794–1813); of superior proportions, the tea or coffeepots present a further elaboration of the concave-shoulder form, with a complexity that prefigures the Empire period. The shape of the carved wooden handles should be noted; conventionally scroll-shaped, they have bold leaf-grips and are made very thin just above the lower socket, to further the visual effect of lightness. A concave shoulder similar, but not nearly so bold, is seen on the sugar urn by Daniel Dupuy, Jr. (1717–1807), who also made the conventional pitcher. Tongs of the spring kind rather than the earlier scissor-form, by Joseph Richardson, Jr., add a final touch to the set.

The composite New York tea set *(Fig. 200)* by William G. Forbes is not notable for especial elegance. However, the coffeepot and sugar urn are unusual shapes, not otherwise seen here. The urn is a variant of the basic boat-shape *(see Fig. 195),* with heavy gadroons (rather than flutes) on the sides toward each end of the body and cover, and ring handles. While the teapot and cream jug also have the gadroon motif, the coffeepot is so large that the silversmith lightened it visually with a broad, shallow flute, the inversion of the gadroon. An unusual and pleasing combination of boat-shape and urn-form, the coffeepot is over twelve inches high. All the objects are decorated with typical New York bright-cutting.

A superb tea set by Ephraim Brasher *(Figs. 201, 202, and 203)* epitomizes the best New York qualities of design and decoration. Relatively standard in form—with the exception of the fine cover on the sugar urn—the set is enlivened with detail of the most exquisite kind; bright-cutting, beading (especially successful on the handle of the cream jug), and cast finials. The elegant proportions are especially noteworthy.

The finest kind of tea set from Boston was undoubtedly made by Revere; the superb example shown here *(Fig. 204)* was fashioned for John Templeman of Boston ten years after his marriage in 1783 and is the only Revere tea set known to have survived complete. The teapot rests on a richly engraved matching stand (to keep heat away from polished wooden surfaces); the caddy, which is identical to the body of the teapot, also has a stand. The cream jug is tall, delicate, and elegant for its form, while the sugar urn is characteristically broad. Typical Revere bright-cutting appears on each piece. A strainer identical to the type used earlier for punch bowls, a small, enchanting shell-shaped caddy spoon, and long, elegant sugar tongs with shell-shaped grips complete the set.

Most of the coffeepots of the early classical period are urn-shaped, with a high concave collar and a similarly shaped

199

200

cover that is domed and surmounted by an urn-finial. One such, splendid in its great size and intricate detail, epitomizes the form *(Fig. 205)*. Made by John Germon of Philadelphia, it is ornamented with a cipher in a classical cartouche and many bands of beading, some of which (on the foot of the pot and on the finial) are swirled. The beading on the spout, with its long juncture, and the intricate, scrolled handle, with its elaborate junctures, enhance this superb object.

An unusual survival of the pear-shaped form may be seen on an imposing coffee-pot *(Fig. 206)* by John Vernon of New York (worked *ca.* 1787–1816). What reveals its classical origin (despite the body shape and the double-scroll handle of the Rococo style) is the high foot, the horizontal reeding at foot and lip, and the urn finial. Furthermore, the body has the taut surface one expects from classical silver,

rather than the languid, sinuous appearance of earlier periods.

Tankards declined markedly in popularity and number in this period, especially in comparison with the enormous number of classical objects produced for the tea table. Two basic types of tankard were made, one of which shows little change from the form prevalent in the fully developed Rococo period. An example of this type was made about 1790 by Joseph Foster of Boston (1760–1837) for presentation to the South Church in Ipswich, Massachusetts *(Fig. 207)*. Compared to the earlier Revere tankard at Yale *(see Fig. 140)* one sees little change, except for the bright-cut classical swags and the slightly higher domed cover—a feature that was accentuated at this time.

The second kind of tankard is more typical of the classical style *(Fig. 208)*. The almost straight cylindrical body displays a very simple baseband, and is decorated with two broad areas of horizontal reeding, reminiscent of a barrel body; such tankards are often called "hooped." Incised rings on the completely flat cover recall the rings on the body. The thumb-piece is a flat, wide strip, often pierced in a delicate pattern, while the handle is a reduced, flatter, and quite unattractive version of the double-scroll. Yet the refinement of outline and proportion, and the

183

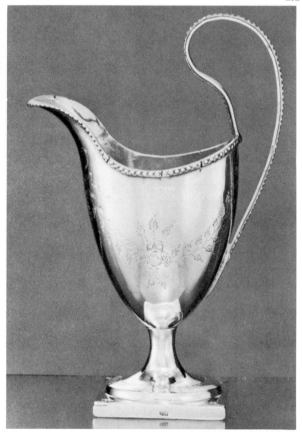

204

205

201. Teapot, *ca.* 1790–1800, by Ephraim Brasher; H. 5¾ inches. Yale University Art Gallery, New Haven, Connecticut. The Mabel Brady Garvan Collection.

202. Cream jug, *ca.* 1790–1800, by Ephraim Brasher; H. 6¹⁵⁄₁₆ inches. Yale University Art Gallery, New Haven, Connecticut. The Mabel Brady Garvan Collection.

203. Sugar urn, *ca.* 1790–1800, by Ephraim Brasher; H. 7½ inches. Yale University Art Gallery, New Haven, Connecticut. The Mabel Brady Garvan Collection.

204. Tea set, 1792–93, by Paul Revere; H. (urn) 9⅝ inches. The Minneapolis Institute of Arts. Gift of Mr. and Mrs. James Ford Bell.

205. Coffeepot, *ca.* 1790–1800, by John Germon; H. 15¹³⁄₁₆ inches. Yale University Art Gallery, New Haven, Connecticut. The Mabel Brady Garvan Collection.

206

207

208

206. Coffeepot, *ca.* 1790–1800, by John Vernon; H. 14¾ inches. Yale University Art Gallery, New Haven, Connecticut. The Mabel Brady Garvan Collection.

207. Tankard, *ca.* 1787–90, by Joseph Foster; H. 8¾ inches. Yale University Art Gallery, New Haven, Connecticut. The Mabel Brady Garvan Collection.

208. Tankard, *ca.* 1790, by Joseph Lownes; H. 7¾ inches. Owned by The Henry Ford Museum, Dearborn, Michigan.

---

lack of ostentatious curves on the body are fully typical of the classical aesthetic. As with many of the pieces we have already seen in this chapter, this tankard (by Joseph Lownes) was presented to a sea captain; a ship is engraved within the elaborate bright-cut cartouche (somewhat Rococo in outline although composed of classical elements).

Most classical canns are similar to the Lownes tankard in style, having straight sides, reeded decoration, and a rather cramped handle. Large pitchers, with or without covers, were also made, reminiscent of the Liverpool creamware jug *(see Fig. 197)*, often with "hooped" rings on the sides.

The difference between classical and fully developed Rococo ideals is well illustrated by a comparison of the sauceboat *(Fig. 209)* by Joseph Anthony, Jr. (1762–1814) with the earlier Burt example *(see Fig. 136)*. The similarities between the two objects serve to highlight the real differences. Both have a Rococo type of high-arched handle and beading,

209

210

and the bodies are alike. But the later example stands on a single splayed foot rather than three scroll or cabriole legs. The resulting solidity, together with the more contained proportions of the body and the less insistent rhythms of the beading, combine to give the Philadelphia sauceboat not the vivid movement of the earlier piece but rather a superb classical poise.

Cups and beakers—small, unpretentious objects—lent themselves well to the classical aesthetic. The pair of cups made by Revere in 1796 for the Honorable Artemas Ward's gift to the Church of Christ in Shrewsbury, Massachusetts, are of typical half-urn shape on a very tall splayed foot *(Fig. 210)*. Ephraim Brasher of New York made a similar pair, with reeded molding on the foot, for presentation to the Congregational Church in Medway, Georgia, ten years earlier (now in the Flemington Presbyterian Church, Hinesville, Georgia). Extremely simple and extremely beautiful, Revere's cups are far more successful than a beaker made by the same silversmith for the First Church in New Yarmouth, Maine, in 1795 *(Fig. 211)*. The body of the beaker (still in transition between the inverted-bell shape of the Rococo and the classical urn shape) is not nearly so well proportioned as that of the cups. It certainly cannot compete in restraint and purity with the small beaker shown in Figure 212. Made by Ebenezer Chittenden (1726–1812) of New Haven, Connecticut in 1792, its proportions (note the close ratio of neck width to base width), its simple decoration, and its lettering are all perfectly harmonious and perfectly in accord with the classical taste.

By the end of the Rococo period, spoons were being made with backward-bent handle-ends and were often decorated on the front of the handle with bright-cutting. This fashion continued into the classical period. Frequently there was a short midrib added to the back of the handle, and

211

209. Sauceboat, *ca.* 1790–1800, by Joseph Anthony, Jr.; H. 5½ inches. Courtesy of The Detroit Institute of Arts.

210. Pair of cups, 1796, by Paul Revere; H. 6⁵⁄₁₆ inches. First Congregational Church, Shrewsbury, Massachusetts. Photograph courtesy of Worcester Art Museum, Worcester, Massachusetts.

211. Beaker, 1795, by Paul Revere; H. 5½ inches. Yale University Art Gallery, New Haven, Connecticut. The Mabel Brady Garvan Collection.

the bowl of the spoon became longer. The drop on the back of the bowl at the stem might take the form of an acanthus leaf or dove holding an olive branch, in relief. An example by Revere *(Fig. 213)*,

189

made for the silversmith Josiah Austin of Boston to retail, shows two further distinguishing features of the period: a slender fluted bowl, and a shoulder on the handle just above the bowl. This example illustrates the excellence of Revere's bright-cut designs. At the beginning of the new century, a graceful spoon-design appeared, lugubriously termed "coffin-end" *(Fig. 214)*; the end of the backward-bent handle was squared off. Completely in accord with the classical taste for smooth, uninterrupted surfaces, these objects are often extremely attractive.

212

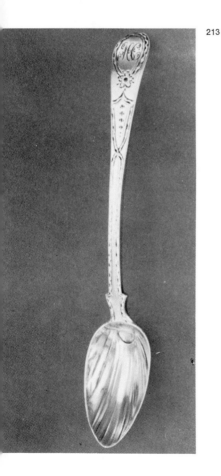

213

214

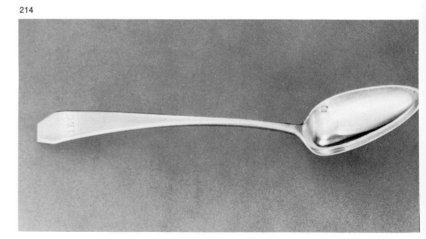

212. Beaker, 1792, by Ebenezer Chittenden; H. 4³⁄₁₆ inches. Yale University Art Gallery, New Haven, Connecticut. The Mabel Brady Garvan Collection.

213. Spoon, 1787, by Paul Revere; L. 5³⁄₈ inches. Yale University Art Gallery, New Haven, Connecticut. Gift of Josephine Setze for The John Marshall Phillips Collection.

214. Spoon, *ca.* 1805–15, by Isaac Hutton; L. 9⁷⁄₁₆ inches. Yale University Art Gallery, New Haven, Connecticut. The Mabel Brady Garvan Collection.

215. Presentation vase, 1812–13, by Fletcher and Gardiner; H. 28 inches. Naval Historical Foundation, Washington, D.C. Photograph courtesy of United States Navy.

CHAPTER SEVEN

The Empire Style

215

In the second and third decades of the nineteenth century, the Empire or fully developed classical style was paramount. It was the apotheosis of the classicizing, archaeologically oriented taste that swept Europe and America from the end of the eighteenth century to about the middle of the nineteenth. Growing accumulations of the visual evidence of antiquity prompted designers and craftsmen to ever more complex incorporation into their works of a variety of classical motifs, often more or less indiscriminately culled from Egypt, Greece, and Rome. In Europe, the more ambitious silver forms of these years were frequently designed by artists and architects, such as John Flaxman and Charles Percier, and subsequently executed by silversmiths. European fashions remained the paragon for taste in America, and the influence of the leading European silversmiths—Paul Storr of the Regency period in England, and Martin Guillaume Biennais of the Consulate and Empire periods in France—was as strong as ever.

This period saw Charles Bulfinch designing buildings in Washington, William Strickland in Philadelphia, Ithiel Town in New Haven and New York, and the grand plans of Thomas Jefferson. It saw the completion of John Trumbull's great series of historical paintings celebrating the nascent republic—a series that had changed in mid-course from Baroque to classical pictorial styles. John Vanderlyn returned from Paris full of the tenets of classicism. Duncan Phyfe and the French immigrant Charles-Honoré Lannuier in New York brought a rare accumulation of classical detail, in both wood and metal, to American furniture. America's friendship with France, as a result of its support during the Revolutionary War, was given tremendous impetus by the war with England from 1812 to 1814 (although it is notable that Sheraton's later, fully developed classical designs were published in England in 1812 and were important in influ-

encing taste in America). This short war may be satisfactorily regarded as the beginning of the Empire period, prompting as it did an important series of documented presentation pieces of silver, all in the latest style.

During this period, New York thoroughly established its pre-eminence as the leading city in America. By 1830, its population of over two hundred thousand far exceeded that of Philadelphia, with one hundred and sixty thousand, and of Boston, with only sixty thousand. Its export and import trade by 1830 was three times greater than that of its nearest competitor; this superiority is not necessarily reflected, however, in the amount or quality of its silver compared with Philadelphia.

The industrial revolution in America in the nineteenth century inevitably led to the erosion of old patterns and values in society, particularly those involving the crafts, trades, and skills. Increasing usage of a wide variety of machines led to the beginnings of mass production; the change from custom-made to wholesale-order work in this period is fully apparent. Obviously, this also spelled the decline of the apprenticeship and indentured-service systems. Notable in this period is the establishment of firms or small factories for the making of silver articles, mainly tea and dinner services, and a decrease in the number of identifiable individual silversmiths. Increasingly, silversmiths of this time made use of journeymen and firms specializing in merchandising silver and other luxury items. Some of the leading silversmiths of the classical period never actually made silver but instead employed a number of craftsmen in their firms. An increasing part of their business was making silver for retailers (marked with the retailers' marks) in the provincial cities that sprang up as the frontiers of America pushed further westward. (In this they followed the custom of John Hull in the seventeenth century, who presumably employed several workmen; and also the documented practice of Paul Revere, who made silver for silversmiths outside Boston and put their marks on it.)

Society retained its preference for the taut surfaces of the early classical fashion, and the urn- or boat-shaped forms so popular then, but it demanded that they be appreciably heavier in weight and proportion and virtually buried under a mass of the most finely and intricately executed detail. Most of this detail was cast, rather than chased as it had been in earlier periods, and much of it had a machine-like smoothness.

Many of the fine pieces of the early classical period had been inscribed as gifts, commemorating significant events on a personal or local level. In the Empire period, the immediacy of the war with England raised the use of presentation silver to a national level. Naval heroes of the various skirmishes between the two countries were handsomely rewarded by the increasingly prosperous populace with meticulously inscribed pieces of plate in the latest fashion. Among the craftsmen affected by this euphoria, the firm of Thomas Fletcher and Sidney Gardiner, active in Philadelphia from 1812 to about 1838, secured a large proportion of the commissions.

We have already discussed one of the earliest classical presentation urns, made about 1800 by Joseph Lownes (see Fig. 194). Elements of the form and decoration definitely suggest the Empire period—the eagle finial, the knopped stem, the elaborate and heavy band of naturalistic decoration (in this instance engraved) at the lip of the body. However, the relative purity of profile of the object defines it as early classical in style, compared to the earliest known Fletcher and Gardiner presentation urn (Fig. 215). One of the first and perhaps the most famous of the naval actions of the war precipitated

the gift of this huge urn or vase from the citizens of Philadelphia to Captain Isaac Hull, in 1812–13. Loosely derived from the ancient Greek ceramic form (the krater), via Paris and the embellishments of designers such as Percier and Pierre Fontaine, the urn is the essence of what to modern eyes seems the traditional kind of trophy.

The body is approximately trumpet-shaped—the broad, round focal band of the piece quickly narrowing down to a thin collar, then flaring out to a round splayed foot set on a square base, supported by a large lion's paw at each corner. Below the main band, the body is heavily decorated with a variety of acanthus-leaf motifs, while the focal level is profusely ornamented with figures in relief, a shallow-relief scene of the naval action surmounted by dolphins, and large, reeded, fixed bail-type handles with ram's-head terminals. The shallow cover has a slight acanthus-leaf dome but is dominated by an eagle with outstretched wings as the finial.

How far from the refined forms and pure profiles of the early classical period! Yet there are premonitions of the new style in certain objects made then (see Fig. 179); the aggregation of fine detail into a profuse elaboration of germane decorative motifs is common to both these pieces. It is the large scale and the obvious boldness of the details of the later urn that mark the obvious difference between the two periods.

By far the most monumental example of the urn-form made by the accomplished firm of Fletcher and Gardiner is the pair of De Witt Clinton vases of 1825 (Fig. 216). Originally designed for a competition organized by a group of New York merchants who wished to express their gratitude to Governor De Witt Clinton for his role in the completion of the Erie Canal, the vases were subsequently commissioned from the silversmiths for pre-

216

216. Presentation vase, 1825, by Fletcher and Gardiner; H. 24 inches. The Chamber of the State of New York. Photograph courtesy of The Metropolitan Museum of Art, New York.

217. Presentation vase, 1830, by Fletcher and Gardiner; H. 21 inches. Yale University Art Gallery, New Haven, Connecticut. Gift of Joseph Brenauer.

217

218

sentation to the governor. Of majestic size (weighing over four hundred ounces each), these objects superbly illustrate the qualities of boldness, vigor, profuse and precise classicizing detail, and monumental scale of the best objects of the Empire period. Very closely derived from an antique prototype (the famous and widely copied "Warwick" vase, a superb marble urn of the second century A.D., found in 1770 near Hadrian's villa at Tivoli, and beautifully engraved in several views by Piranesi in 1778), it is one of the most unified of all Fletcher and Gardiner's creations. The vase differs from its antique prototype mainly in the details of the base, the high foot, and the addition of a cover—apart from the obvious difference in the decorative, emblematic motifs on the sides of the body. The egg-and-dart motifs, the handles, the grapes and vine leaves at the rim, and the human masks are all based on the antique. The typical Fletcher and Gardiner base (here simple but very pow-

218. Inkstand, ca. 1815–25, by Harvey Lewis; H. 3⅝ inches. Yale University Art Gallery, New Haven, Connecticut. The Mabel Brady Garvan Collection.

erful) and the tall foot actually provide a highly satisfactory visual support for the mass of the body, while the cover and eagle finial provide an appropriate apex to the design. The twisted vine-stem handles, with their intricate detail and intense movement, supply a strong accent at a crucial point in the design. Close examination of the details, including views of the significant parts of the canal and representations of the Sciences, Fame, and History reveal the silversmiths' striking virtuosity. These vases (or two-handled covered cups) are as splendid and important in their period as other two-handled covered cups are in almost all of the preceding style periods.

196

Near the end of its working period, in 1830, the firm of Fletcher and Gardiner made another massive two-handled covered vase, occasioned this time by the retirement of the President of the Chesapeake and Delaware Canal Company. (Gardiner died in 1827; presumably, Fletcher was the master designer and silversmith of the partnership.) Similar in scale to the preceding objects, this vase *(Fig. 217)* lacks their linear grace and formal strength. The high, square base dominates the bulbous body, while the handles are too small to provide an appropriate accent of strength at the main focal point. Nor does the brilliant detail mask these differences; indeed, it tends to exaggerate the formal imbalances.

In marked contrast to these massive objects is a small masterpiece by Harvey Lewis of Philadelphia (worked *ca.* 1811–25). Although diminutive in size, this inkstand *(Fig. 218)* is typical of the period in its employment of abundant, precise detail, such as that found on the huge vases. The body is hemispherical, with a small reel-shaped appendage below, supported on a tri-cornered plinth by three legs in the form of winged sphinxes terminating in paws. Appliqués of flowers and leaves can be seen on the body and the plinth, which are also decorated with beaded leaf-bands. Each sphinx has a beaded acanthus ornament in the form of a headdress, presumably to hold quills. The profusion of French-inspired antique detail and the classicizing form combine to give this small object extraordinary visual strength.

Perhaps the most intrinsically elegant and splendid objects of this period *(Fig. 219)* were also made in Philadelphia at this time by the French immigrant Anthony Rasch (worked *ca.* 1807–25). The long, slim, languid body of the sauceboat is set on the kind of foot and base seen frequently in this period, supported by four tiny winged lions. The handle is

brilliantly devised in the form of an undulating snake, while the pouring lip is heavily decorated with a bull's head. The beaded leaf border of the rim has already been seen on the Lewis inkstand. For their flair and grace, their preciousness, their ingenuity and quality of execution, these sauceboats are exceptional.

A vivid counterpoint to the Lewis inkstand is a rare example of the form *(Fig. 220)* from Boston, made by Obadiah Rich (worked *ca.* 1830–50). This comparison further illuminates the kind of contrast we have seen in the work of the two cities throughout our period. For its effect, the northern example relies upon a lean but forceful line and subdued decoration. Here the plinth is undecorated and the slender urn-shaped body plain except for the boldly scrolled legs, which open into foliage and dogs' heads; even the rim of the body is merely marked with a milled flange rather than an elaborate beaded band. Yet its restraint is a virtue, for the line is superb and the detail fully equal to the exceptional standards of the Empire period.

Boston silver of this period is scarce. Rich (working for the firm of Jones, Ball, and Low) made an almost literal copy of the Warwick vase *(Fig. 221)*, although he transformed the human masks into animal heads, surrounded by animal skins and large clusters of grapes. This large vase was presented to Daniel Webster by the citizens of Boston in 1835 and is notable for its closeness to the antique prototype, as well as for its commanding size and rarity.

Probably the grandest virtuoso effect in silver of these years was achieved in the huge two-handled vase presented by a group of New York merchants to District Attorney Hugh Maxwell in 1829 *(Fig. 222)*. It was made by Baldwin Gardiner (worked *ca.* 1827–38), who, as the brother of one of the partners, had been associated with the firm of Fletcher and Gardi-

219

219. Pair of sauceboats, *ca.* 1815–20, by Anthony Rasch; L. 11¾₁₆ inches. The Metropolitan Museum of Art, New York. Fletcher Fund, 1959.

220. Inkstand, *ca.* 1830, by Obadiah Rich; H. 3⅝ inches. Yale University Art Gallery, New Haven, Connecticut. The Mabel Brady Garvan Collection.

221. Presentation vase, 1835, by Obadiah Rich; H. 15 inches. Boston Public Library.

220

221

222

222. Presentation vase, 1829, by Baldwin
Gardiner; H. 24½ inches. The New York Law
Institute. Photograph courtesy of The New-York
Historical Society, New York City.

ner in Philadelphia for some years before his removal to New York. In some ways it is even more closely modeled on the Warwick vase than the De Witt Clinton vases of similar size—in the shape of the foot and the acanthus-leaf decoration on the base of the body. But it lacks the massive unity and force of the earlier vases; its effect is too dispersed and the motifs too various. The body and foot are of superb quality and more unified than those elements of the De Witt Clinton vases—the bands of ornament on a grand scale commensurate with the size and shape of the object, and the main focal band of the body not cluttered with the relief decoration of the earlier examples. Yet the bold acanthus-and-paw feet and sphinxes of the tripod stand, the detail of which is extraordinary, are so overelaborate as to throw the whole design into disunity.

One of the monuments of this period, in its grand size and ambitious design, is the plateau by John W. Forbes of New York (ca. 1781–ca. 1838), now in the White House (Figs. 223 and 224). According to tradition, it was ordered from Forbes about 1804, although this seems too early in the century if one considers the dates of the Fletcher and Gardiner presentation pieces. (Moreover, a virtually identical example by the same maker was presented by the citizens of the State of New York to De Witt Clinton in 1825.) The large plateau was designed to stand in the center of the dining-room table and serve as a base for condiments and the various silver and glass accessories of the service. To add to the impression of richness, the bottom was mirrored. The pierced vertical rim of the plateau is a tour de force of typical Empire motifs—rich acanthus-leaf and naturalistic decoration, winged lions, and urns and wreaths. Over each of the six acanthus-leaf legs and paws is a vertical accent, a plaque of a classical goddess in relief, with an eagle finial. Its size, richness, and exotic purpose combine to symbolize the pride and ambition of the increasingly prosperous merchant class of the young Republic.

Almost contemporary with the Hull urn of 1812–13 (see Fig. 215) are two urns or vases made to commemorate the naval heroics of Captain Jacob Jones. One of these was commissioned from Fletcher and Gardiner by the Legislature of the State of Delaware (Fig. 225); the other from Simon Chaudron of Philadelphia (worked ca. 1798–1825) by the citizens of Philadelphia (Fig. 226). Both objects reveal the dangers facing silversmiths who exerted a less than rigid control over profile and the use of decoration. The Fletcher and Gardiner example is characterized by a rotundity of form and bulkiness of proportion frequently seen in this period. Sharing many formal details with the Hull urn, the Jones vase also has a broad focal band, with appropriate marine motifs; but this is set on a bulbous body that is itself decorated, on the lower part, with a band of acanthus leaves. Base, handles, and cover are similar to the Hull urn, yet the piece lacks the obvious symmetry and the clear profile of the earlier urn. The example by Chaudron, who had emigrated to Philadelphia from France, is closer still to the Hull urn, although the body is more hemispherical. Again, the decoration of acanthus leaves, masks, and a figure of victory surmounting the cover is exquisite in execution but excessive in proportion. Indeed, on the base it is also excessive in quantity, so that the whole object appears ponderous.

During these years, silversmiths in England and France frequently utilized the body form of the Warwick vase for wine coolers, without covers and often without handles. The shape was also slightly changed so that the lower, convex part of the belly was more pronounced, and the surmounting concave area pinched further in, giving the whole a primarily vertical

223

224

223. Plateau, *ca.* 1820–30, by John W. Forbes; L. *ca.* 64 inches. White House Collection.

224. Detail of Fig. 223.

225. Presentation vase, 1813–14, attributed to Fletcher and Gardiner; H. 16 inches. By courtesy of the Historical Society of Delaware.

226. Presentation vase, 1813, by Simon Chaudron; H. 16½ inches. Courtesy of The New-York Historical Society, New York City.

225

226

227

227. Presentation vase, 1828, by Baldwin Gardiner; H. 18 inches. Courtesy of The New-York Historical Society, New York City.

228. Pitcher, 1813, by Simon Chaudron; H. 16 inches. Courtesy of The New-York Historical Society, New York City.

---

aspect. Although this form was used much less frequently in America, several examples have survived. One excellent piece is replete with cover *(Fig. 227)*, but it well illustrates the successful profile achieved by varying the proportions of the Warwick vase. The bold acanthus-leaf ornament on the belly, the strong foot, and the delicate scroll handles together attain a fine harmony. There is sufficient plain surface to balance the rich detail, which is characteristically superb in execution: the Neptune masks at the lower juncture of the handles and the decoration on top of the cover are especially fine. This covered urn or vase was made by Baldwin Gardiner in 1828 for presentation to Henry Eckford of New York by his fellow citizens.

Urns were not the only objects to be used for presentation purposes in these years, though their documented origin, large size, and great weight often endow them with importance and monumentality. Large ewers or pitchers were frequently given, together with urns or by themselves and could be strikingly elegant. The first such pitcher illustrated here

(Fig. 228) was designed to accompany a large urn. Made by Simon Chaudron for presentation to Captain James Lawrence in 1813 by the citizens of Philadelphia, its derivation from earlier classical pitchers is obvious *(see Fig. 177)*. The urn- or helmet-shaped body is, however, enriched at the bottom with broad gadrooning and acanthus leaves interspersed with spears; the delicate detail on the foot and the neck, and the marine motifs are typical of Empire silver. The high arched handle is

one of the few touches of sweeping movement and grace on what is otherwise a dignified and solid-looking object.

Typical Empire proportions characterize the rotund body of the pitcher *(Fig. 229)* presented to President Madison about 1809. Made by Ward and Bartholomew of Hartford, Conn. (worked *ca.* 1804–9), it must be one of the earliest pieces of silver in this style, although it can hardly be considered outstanding either in outline or in detail. The feet in the form of winged animals (obviously developed from the ball feet widely used in the preceding style period), the broad band of leaves at the base of the body, and the animal head on the handle are all motifs characteristic of this period. How much more graceful is the example made two decades later by Baldwin Gardiner *(Fig. 230)* for presentation to Commodore Isaac Chauncey in 1833 by the citizens of Brooklyn! Only the thin handle of this slender and elegant piece may be faulted: Although it conveys a perfect sense of movement, it appears to lack sufficient weight. Precise details do not become oppressive by repetition or weight, nor do they obscure the excellent proportions, profile, and balance of the pitcher.

In their developing boldness and rotundity, early classical forms for the tea table obviously prefigure Empire shapes. The first service illustrated here *(Fig. 231)* has the surface simplicity of the early classical period but the bold, rounded forms and the complex feet and finials of the later period. It bears the date 1810 and was made by William Thompson of New York (worked 1809–45). We have already seen a rotund body of this kind *(see Fig. 189)*, obviously derived from the early classical oval boat-shaped form. Ball feet first appeared around the turn of the century and were popular for some years; this service combines ball feet with ball-and-claw (an alternative to the animal forms we have already seen in this chap-

228

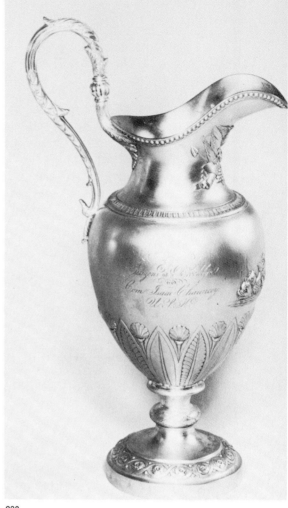

229   230

229. Pitcher, *ca.* 1804–9, by Ward and Bartholomew; H. 13⅜ inches. Courtesy of The New-York Historical Society, New York City.

230. Pitcher, 1833, by Baldwin Gardiner; H. 17 inches. Courtesy of The New-York Historical Society, New York City.

231. Tea set, 1810, by William Thompson; H. (teapot) 9¾ inches. The Philip H. Hammerslough Collection. Photograph courtesy of Wadsworth Atheneum, Hartford, Connecticut.

232. Teapot, *ca.* 1810–20, by Charles A. Burnett; H. 9½ inches. The Philip H. Hammerslough Collection. Photograph courtesy of Wadsworth Atheneum, Hartford, Connecticut.

231

232

233

234

ter). Its attractive simplicity is complemented by such fine details as the gadrooning and the shape of the handles.

Broadly fluted forms also occur in both the early and later classical periods. A striking example *(Fig. 232)* by Charles A. Burnett of Alexandria, Virginia (1785–1849), is further embellished with a rich flourish of animal forms at spout and handle. The slim, square base for the foot derives from early classical urn-shaped forms, but the bands of crisscross ornament on the body and the rather beautifully fluted cover are imaginative touches characteristic of the best Empire silver.

It is a short step from this example to the fully orchestrated Empire tea set *(Fig. 233)* by William Seal of Philadelphia (worked *ca.* 1816–20). Seal utilized the same broad, rounded body as did Burnett *(see Fig. 232)*, and similar bands of ornament on the foot and near the cover as did William Thompson *(see Fig. 231);* but instead of ball feet there are owls with outstretched wings. A band of machine-rolled basket-weave ornament on the bodies constitutes a further enrichment. The handles of the teapot and cream jug are ornamented; the spout of the teapot is in the familiar animal form, and there are rams' heads applied at the lips of the sugar and slop bowls. The plain domed covers are surmounted by large swan finials.

It was only too easy for the silversmith to attempt to integrate a large number of motifs into a homogeneous form and fail miserably. The teapot by William Thompson *(Fig. 234)*, made for presentation to Captain William Bowne of the ship *Courier* in 1819, is such an instance. It is a foretaste of the worst excesses of the nineteenth century. The bulbous body sags between unfortunate bird-form legs, while the handle—not notably different from those we have already seen in this chapter —adds the extra decorative touch that is least needed for this particular piece.

235

236

237

236. Teapot, *ca.* 1820–28, by William B. Heyer; H. 10½ inches. Yale University Art Gallery, New Haven, Connecticut. Gift of Mrs. William Crozier and William Williams in memory of their grandmother, Lucretia Woodbridge Williams.

237. Sugar bowl, *ca.* 1820–28, by William B. Heyer; H. 9⁵⁄₁₆ inches. Yale University Art Gallery, New Haven, Connecticut. Gift of Mrs. William Crozier and William Williams in memory of their grandmother, Lucretia Woodbridge Williams.

The kind of scrolled foliate band on the shoulder of the Thompson teapot could be used to different effect in this period, as, for example, on a tea and coffee service by Simon Chaudron (*Fig. 235*). Larger in scale here, it forms the main focal point of each object, although its machine-made symmetry is not particularly appealing. In form, the set is reminiscent of the Fletcher and Gardiner vase presented to Captain Jacob Jones (*see Fig. 225*), where the main focal band surmounts a bulbous body. It is not a successful design. Though forthright and finely executed, it is strangely lacking in grace.

Less ambitious in design, imbued with a naïve yet forceful quality is a tea set (*Figs. 236 and 237*) by William B. Heyer of New York (1776–1828). Its formal elements are similar to the Chaudron set, with the further addition of large-scale gadrooning—the decorative band at the shoulder is the focal point of each piece. In this instance, the band is composed of rustic scenes in shallow relief. Square handles, plain spout, and the repetition of the gadrooning, in miniature, on the cover all enhance these vigorous objects.

Among the numerous Empire pieces designed for the dinner table two handsome forms stand out and are illustrated here. The large covered tureen (*Fig. 238*) is very unusual in American silver; made by Hugh Wishart of New York (worked *ca.* 1784–1816), it was destined for Robert Lenox of New York and bears his crest. It is actually one of a set of three, the other two being smaller and probably intended for sauce or vegetables. Its plain surfaces would seem to place it firmly in the earlier classical period (a supposition that the working dates of the silversmith would confirm), yet the bulbous, rounded forms and the handles with foliage have a definite Empire quality to them. Also typical of the period are the decorated bands seen here on the body of a small but heavy tankard—an unusual form at

this time—made by Fletcher and Gardiner (*Fig. 239*). The slightly domed cover and the simple thumbpiece and handle are obviously developments from the earlier classical style (*see Fig. 208*).

Samuel Kirk (1793–1872) began producing idiosyncratic silver in Baltimore in this period—an activity that has been maintained through various generations of the family to the present. Combined with a predilection for some of the more exotic forms of these years was Kirk's devotion to a plethora of intricate detail; the results were distinctive and frequently highly unpleasant. A salver or tray (*Fig. 240*) made in 1828 is a good illustration; the basic form is enriched with swirled gadrooning, and the face with punched designs frequently employed in Europe in the classical period. Added to all this (sufficient in itself), is a "crazed" design within the gadrooning, and then a chased floral design, with scrolls and houses, inside that. The final touch is a shield and crest within a vine-and-grape cartouche.

While such objects as mugs, cups, and porringers—popular in previous periods—were rarely made in the nineteenth century, spoons were produced in plentiful numbers. There was also a corresponding rise in the number of flatware services with knives, forks, and spoons, all of different sizes for various functions. Empire flatware was characteristically "fiddle-end" in this period—that is, flattened somewhat like a spatula and backward-bent. It was often decorated on the front with a stamped sheaf of wheat, basket, or shell design in relief. By the end of the period, the handle-end became forward-bent, and the sides were curved in and out, so that it more closely resembled the body of a violin. This type is termed "wavy fiddle-end." Handles were often stamped with a lined border or relief decoration. This remained the basic pattern for an infinite number of variables for most of the century.

238

238. Tureen, *ca.* 1810–15, by Hugh Wishart; H. 4½ inches. Courtesy of The New-York Historical Society, New York City.

239. Tankard, *ca.* 1815–25, by Fletcher and Gardiner; H. 4¾ inches. Collection of Mr. and Mrs. Denison H. Hatch, Riverside, Connecticut. Photograph courtesy of Gebelein Silversmiths, Boston.

240. Tray, *ca.* 1828, by Samuel Kirk; D. 8 inches. The Metropolitan Museum of Art, New York. Gift of Samuel Kirk and Son, Inc., 1926.

239

240

Expansion—spasmodic but inexorable—is the key word for America from 1830 until the end of the nineteenth century. Population, individual wealth, the purchasing power of the middle classes, industrialization and technology, territorial development and the sense of nationality, combined with an awareness of the incomparable richness of Europe's artistic past and present—all expanded enormously in the nineteenth century. It is symbolic that the second half of the century (the focus of this chapter) began with the discovery of gold in California and ended with the Gilded Age.

Without any doubt, New York became the social and artistic capital of America in this period. This is reflected in the quantity of important pieces illustrated here that were made either in New York or for residents of the city. Philadelphia and Boston certainly had active silversmiths and silver retailers, but they were not especially superior to silversmiths in Baltimore, for example, or to such firms as the Gorham Company in Providence.

The greatly increased numbers and wealth of the middle classes in the nineteenth century created a demand for silver that only mass-production methods could supply. Developed technology in the form of mechanized casting, rolling, and electroplating, and the important discovery in the West of extensive deposits of silver facilitated the large-scale production. The inevitable result, however, was that the silver became progressively impersonal. This state of affairs was not helped by the widespread practice of engaging gifted individuals to design silver, which was later made in a factory by anonymous silversmiths. The increasingly wide division between conception and execution in the silversmithing process thus meant that the actual silversmith in the nineteenth century became, to a great extent, a mere artificer. This division is indelibly reflected in many of the objects themselves.

Later Nineteenth-Century Styles

213

In any event, the stabilization of currencies in the nineteenth century meant that silver occupied a less essential role in society; its former economic importance virtually disappeared, although it was still valued for purposes of ostentation. Indeed, the response of the rich élite to the widespread middle-class desire for silver was a demand for even more ornament and lavishness. Much of the odium later attached to nineteenth-century silver resulted from precisely this excess of machine-made ornament. Movements at the end of the century (the Arts and Crafts Movement and Art Nouveau) were directed primarily at abolishing undue ornament and eliminating the machine from the craft process.

Thus far in the history of American silver we have seen the fullest expressions of particular styles followed by reactionary periods of relative simplicity. This is not the case with the nineteenth-century styles that succeeded the fully developed classical period. For much of the remainder of the century there seems to have been an almost universal abhorrence of a plain surface. Not that such an attitude is necessarily bad; but the predilection for profuse ornamentation was frequently combined with an overfond regard for—and often a complete misunderstanding of—the styles of the past: "'pure Greek' . . . rigidly 'classical' . . . 'antique' . . . 'Pugin' . . . the *Renaissance* . . . . Everyone selects his own style of art, and the choice rests usually in the shallowest individualism . . . . We all agree only in being wretched imitators" (*Journal of Design*, England, 1849).

The primary stylistic modes following the Empire period were the Rococo revival, which lasted approximately three decades (to about 1860); the Renaissance revival, which survived until about 1880; the Oriental or Moorish vogue merging with Beaux-Arts styles, which flourished up to the last decade of the century; and finally Art Nouveau. But it must be understood that there was simultaneously a welter of other revivals: Gothic, Greek, Elizabethan, Louis XIV, Louis XV, Louis XVI, Egyptian, as well as an agglomeration of various Near-, Mid-, and Far-Eastern styles. Especially useful in distinguishing the bewildering assortment of these renditions are the catalogues of the large fairs or exhibitions that became popular in these years—in particular the New York Exhibition of 1853 (inspired by the Great Exhibition held at the Crystal Palace, London, in 1851), the International Centennial Exhibition at Philadelphia in 1876, and the World's Columbian Exposition at Chicago in 1893.

Immediately following the Empire period, a version of the French Restauration style appeared (a plain version of Empire styles, to put it simply); the influence of this was more fully felt in furniture than in silver. Michael Allison and Joseph Meeks made furniture of this kind in New York, while Antoine-Gabriel Quervelle and the firm of Joseph Barry were active in Philadelphia. Rococo revival styles became widely popular, and in furniture were employed mainly by Meeks and John Henry Belter in New York (the laminated and carved rosewood furniture of this style is generally associated with the latter). The geometrical, classical motifs of the Renaissance revival and the "neo-grec" style—as opposed to the floridly naturalistic forms of the Rococo revival—were popularized by firms of cabinetmakers and decorators, such as Ringuet LePrince and Marcotte, of Paris and New York, Alexander Roux, Julius Dessoir, and Charles Baudoine in New York, and Auguste Eliaers in Boston. Many American de-

241. Tea urn, 1835, by Forbes and Son; H. 20 inches. Collection of Dr. and Mrs. Gerard L. Eastman. Photograph courtesy of Museum of the City of New York.

signers made frequent trips to France and Germany to select materials and motifs, while the firms engaged in manufacturing silver almost invariably turned to Europe for their chief designers: Tiffany and Company brought Gustav Herter from Germany in 1848, and the Gorham Company engaged Thomas Pairpoint, who came from London via Paris in 1868.

By the 1860's, the reaction against the excessive detail and dull mechanical repetitiveness of the various revivals, inspired and organized by John Ruskin and William Morris in England, resulted in Charles Eastlake's influential *Hints on Household Taste*, first published in England in 1868 and in America in 1872. (Together with this, the spirit of America's Centennial celebration produced a renewed appreciation of Colonial and earlier Old World styles and the inevitable reproductions and free interpretations.) Eastlake applauded straight lines and simple, honest construction, and propounded the intrinsically cherishable qualities of good design and skillful workmanship, even in the smallest objects. Yet the geometrical forms he admired were not totally anathema to the apostles of classicism, who incorporated him into their aesthetic and broadcast their refined classical designs under the banner of Beaux-Arts; moreover, his penchant for small, exquisite detail opened the way for "art furniture," for example, and the introduction of Moorish and Oriental decorative designs overlaid on essentially simple forms. In silver this latter trend came to a climax in the work of Tiffany and Company and their designer, the American Edward Moore. From these essentially linear (if very compact) designs it was a short step to Art Nouveau, in which style Tiffany as well as the Gorham Company excelled.

One of the earliest dated Rococo revival objects in silver is a large tea urn made by Forbes and Son and presented by the Firemen of the City of New York to their trustee, the prominent merchant John W. Degrauw, in 1835 *(Fig. 241)*. Its derivation from classical silver is obvious, both in function *(see Fig. 174)* and in form *(see Fig. 217)*. Despite the appearance of vine, paw, and other naturalistic motifs, however, its decoration betrays an obvious dependence on fully developed Rococo ornamentation *(see Fig. 128)*. Even the curved sides of the base reveal a change from the classical type of urn.

The firm of Fletcher and Gardiner, famous for their Empire-style silver, was able to adapt to the changing styles and produce a complete service in the latest fashion that would have been one of the monuments of this period, had it not been subsequently melted down. Fortunately, drawings by Fletcher of part of the service survive *(Fig. 242)*, giving an excellent idea of the design. The item was aptly described by Philip Hone, the former mayor of New York, in a diary entry for January 27, 1838: "I was shown this afternoon, at the shop of Messrs. Fletcher & Co., in Chestnut Street, the most superb service of plate I ever saw, to be presented by the directors of the old Bank of the United States to Mr. Nicholas Biddle. It is to cost $15,000." The tea set in the drawing is certainly devoid of any dependence on Empire styles, with the possible exception of the pendent anthemions at the neck of each piece. The curvilinear bodies are vaguely reminiscent of Rococo pear-shaped forms, although completely different in proportion. The ornamentation on the handles, covers, and feet is Rococo in style, as is the main band of decoration, which combines asymmetrical scrolls and naturalistic ornament. The service was engraved with an inscription that (to quote Philip Hone again) "recites all his [Biddle's] valuable services to the institution and to the country at large, and among other things his having 'created

242

the best currency in the world.' He deserves all they can do for him, but the world is a big place."

In the 1840's, Empire forms could still be found, however. A superb large pitcher and accompanying tray *(Fig. 243)* made by Bard and Lamont of Philadelphia for presentation to the lawyer David Paul Brown by "the disfranchised citizens of Philadelphia" in 1841, in recognition of his abolitionist work, employs a typical Empire form *(see Fig. 230)* and even some Empire motifs, such as the feet of the tray, and the bands of decoration on the shoulder, the lip of the pitcher, and on the edge of the tray. Allied to this, however, is a band of profuse, chased, Rococo ornamentation on the belly of the pitcher and a swooping Rococo handle of a type

217

243

243. Pitcher and tray, 1841, by Bard and Lamont; H. 16½ inches. The Detroit Institute of
Arts. Beatrice Rogers Bequest Fund.

244. Teakettle on stand, 1850, by John
Chandler Moore for Ball, Tompkins and Black;
H. 17⁵⁄₁₆ inches. The Metropolitan Museum of
Art. Gift of Mrs. F. R. Lefferts, 1969.

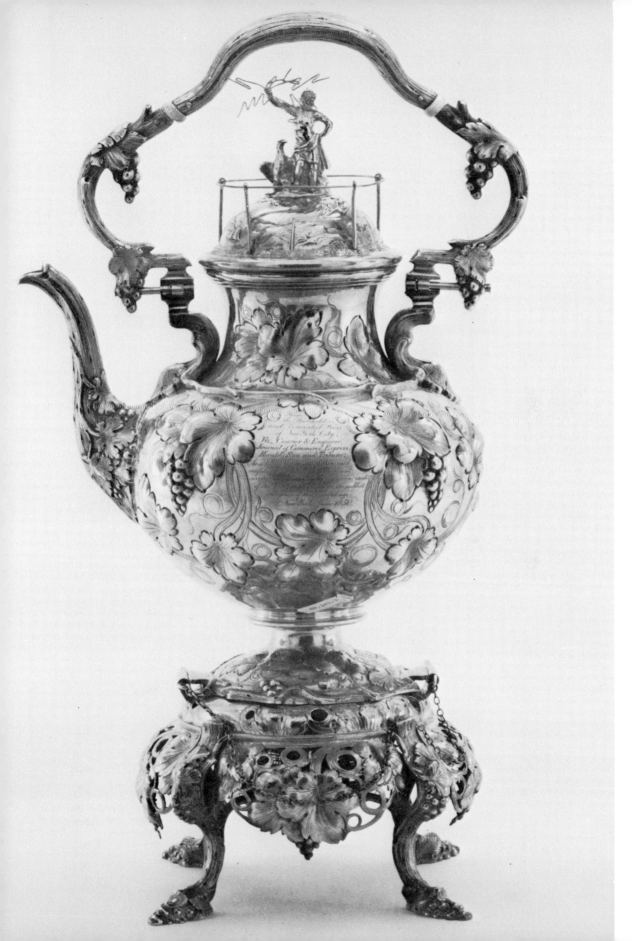

seen only on the best European silver of the mid-eighteenth century. A figure of a kneeling slave giving a prayer of thanks is finely engraved in the reserve on the side of the pitcher opposite the inscription.

By 1850 the Rococo revival was in full cry. An excellent example of the style is a service made for presentation to Marshall Lefferts in 1850, in appreciation of his contribution as head of the company that installed the first telegraph services between New York, Boston, and Buffalo *(Figs. 244 and 245).* It was designed by John Chandler Moore for the New York retailers Ball, Tompkins and Black (this firm became Ball, Black and Company in 1851, and then Black, Starr and Frost in 1876). It is virtually identical to a set (for the same retailers, presumably by the same maker) that was chosen for inclusion in the New York Exhibition of 1853 and that was made entirely of California gold at a cost of five thousand dollars. The similarity in form between the teakettle and its early Rococo relative *(see Fig. 87)* is obvious, yet the later example literally drips with decoration of a most extravagant kind. Not content with a super-abundance of foliage, the designer also embellished the teakettle with scenes of trains and boats, miniature telegraph poles and wires, an eagle, and a benign, electric Zeus. The Rococo revival pitcher is derived from the classical form, but its proportions (as well as its decoration) are changed to suggest something entirely more organic.

Ten years after the Lefferts set was made—the apotheosis of revived Rococo—the Renaissance revival was already under way, as is evident in the splendid tea

---

245. Pitcher, 1850, by John Chandler Moore for Ball, Tompkins and Black; H. 16¼ inches. Museum of the City of New York. Gift of Mrs. Charles S. Stedman, Jr.

and coffee service made by the Gorham Company and presented to Mrs. Abraham Lincoln in 1860 *(Fig. 246).* Classical urn-forms were employed, as well as the beading and lion's masks with bail handles characteristic of classical silver. Yet the decoration has a floridness typical of the mid-nineteenth century, combined with strapwork that was presumably intended to evoke the purity of Renaissance design.

Elements of classical (Greek) origin were often introduced into Renaissance revival designs. Such an amalgam can be seen in a compote *(Fig. 247)* made in 1863 by William Gale and Son of New York (worked *ca.* 1860). The bowl is classical in shape, as are the handles and the Greek fret design. Above the foot is an incongruous square element with a face in relief on each surface.

In contrast to this object is a synthesis of Renaissance revival forms and ornaments that achieves harmony, balance, and poise *(Fig. 248).* The body of this teakettle by Ball, Black and Company of New York, made for presentation to Mary Remsen and Robert Belknap in 1870, echoes the classical urn *(see Fig. 215),* and the legs of the stand, the handle, and the decoration on neck and body invoke strapwork. The repetition of clean profiles and symmetrical balances gives a strong sense of coherence to this design, which is far from the effect achieved by the monument of Renaissance revival in America, the William Cullen Bryant vase of 1874 *(Fig. 249).* To the designer of this elephantine object (James H. Whitehouse for Tiffany and Company), the name of Bryant—to whom the vase was to be presented—evoked "the country . . . and . . . a general contemplation of Nature; and these together with a certain Homeric influence, produced in my mind the germ of the design—the form of a Greek vase, with the most beautiful American flowers and plants growing around and entwining themselves gracefully about it." Such a

221

union of cultures may be thought to have been doomed from the beginning. There is no doubt that, to modern eyes, the latent qualities of form are completely betrayed by the excess of detail, although it was highly regarded at the time as "a combination of simplicity and beauty."

Superbly indicative of the trend against Renaissance formality, which emerged as Moorish or Indian styles not untinged with Art Nouveau, is a small-scale tea set *(Fig. 250)* designed for Tiffany about 1888 by Edward Moore, the son of John Chandler Moore *(see Figs. 244 and 245)*. The objects are as elaborate as the Bryant vase. Not content with the chased decoration, the designer provided etched and gilded surfaces too, in addition to enameling in several colors. Surprisingly, the color of the silver unifies all these motifs, so that the pieces achieve a preciousness and intrinsic richness.

As expressive of the 1890's as the Bryant

vase was of the 1870's is another huge vase *(Fig. 251)* made by Tiffany and Company for the World's Columbian Exposition in 1893. Designed by Edward Moore's successor as chief designer for the firm, John T. Curran, the vase was claimed at the time to be "in its entirety a characteristic American piece." Its form was believed to reflect ancient Pueblo pottery, the handles on the neck being Toltec in derivation and the decoration based on American flowers of all parts of

---

246. Tea and coffee set, 1860, by the Gorham Company; H. (urn) 18 inches. Smithsonian Institution, Washington, D.C.

247. Compote, 1863, by William Gale and Son; W. 10½ inches. The Metropolitan Museum of Art, New York. Anonymous Gift Fund, 1968.

248. Teakettle on stand, *ca.* 1870, by Ball, Black and Company; H. 14¾ inches. Museum of the City of New York. From the collection of Waldron Phoenix Belknap, Jr.

246

247

248

250

249. Vase, 1874, by James H. Whitehouse for Tiffany and Company; H. 33⅜ inches. The Metropolitan Museum of Art, New York. Gift of William Cullen Bryant.

250. Tea set, *ca.* 1888, by Edward Moore for Tiffany and Company; L. (teapot) 11 inches. The Metropolitan Museum of Art, New York. Gift of a friend of the Museum, 1897.

251

251. Vase, 1893, by John T. Curran for Tiffany and Company; H. 31 inches. The Metropolitan Museum of Art, New York. Gift of Mrs. Winthrop Atwell.

252. Pair of vases, 1894, Tiffany and Company; H. 17⅞ inches. Museum of the City of New York. Gift of Harry Harkness Flagler.

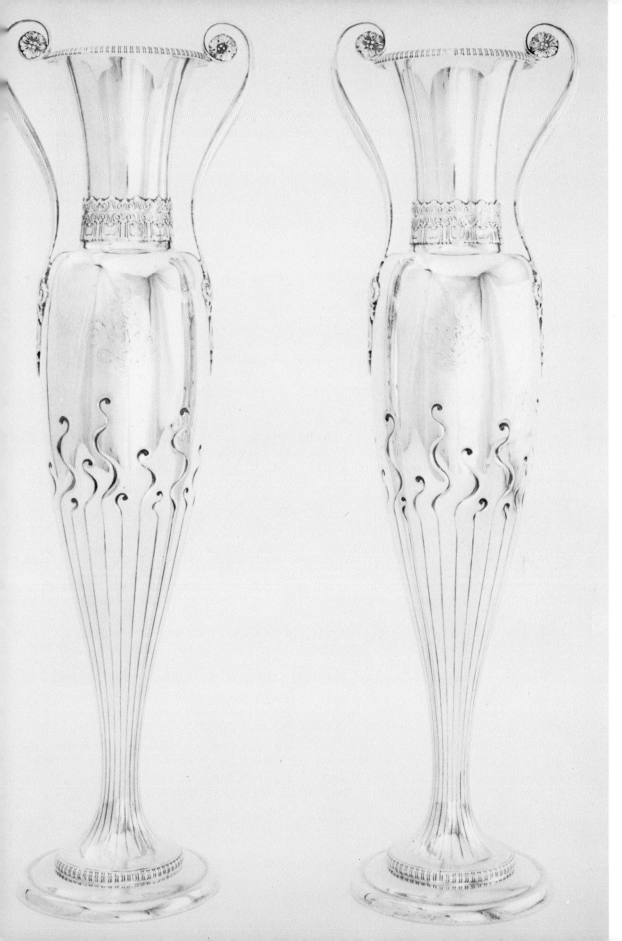

the continent. The flowers on the shoulder of this so-called magnolia vase are profusely enameled, as are the plants on the sides. Its brilliantly executed, exotic, and unbelievably profuse naturalistic decoration make it a monument of the *fin de siècle*.

Infinitely more restrained and elegant, a benign union of the Beaux-Arts tradition and the Art Nouveau style, is the pair of vases made by Tiffany and Company for the wedding of Anne Louise Lamont to Harry Harkness Flagler in 1894 *(Fig. 252)*. From the academic, classical, and Renaissance-inspired tradition of the Parisian Beaux-Arts were derived the shape, the beading, the scroll handles, the rosettes, and the acanthus ornament. Yet the lovely fluid shape, the languorous elegance of the urn, and the incised decoration on the lower part of the body are directly inspired by Art Nouveau.

The grace of Art Nouveau, its viscous liquidity, is perfectly expressed in a punch bowl made from a very pure and soft silver by the Gorham Company *(Fig. 253)*. Though symmetrical, the design is in exemplary Art Nouveau style, with its harmonious undulations suggestive of living and moving organisms. Designed and made from about 1900 onward under the supervision of an English designer, William Codman, expensive objects of this sort made by Gorham were called Martelé.

The pinnacle of the Beaux-Arts tradition in the decorative arts was undoubtedly the Adams vase *(Fig. 254)*, as was, in architecture, the Columbian Exposition in Chicago. Designed by Paulding Farnam for Tiffany and Company in 1891, the vase was presented to Edward Adams, the president of the American Cotton Oil Company for his services in saving his firm from ruin. The serenely classical form of the urn symbolized the virtue and sacrifice of the recipient's labors, and the gold, pearls, semiprecious stones, and wealth of ornamental detail conveyed the donors' magnanimous appreciation. Edward Adams, America, and the overpoweringly individual genius of cotton were all applauded in the overt symbolism of the figures and reliefs on the base and sides. Richly sensuous on the one hand and embarrassingly naïve on the other, the vase itself is a monument of great industry, wealth, and magniloquent moralizing.

Pitchers that combine late classical forms with Rococo revival decoration are among the more satisfying nineteenth-century pieces; the mutual interaction was generally beneficial. One such pitcher, replete with goblets *(Fig. 255)*, retained Empire decorative bands and acanthus leaf but incorporated large Rococo swirls of chased and engraved foliage. The maker, William Adams (worked 1831–50) also incorporated pendent grape-clusters into the design—a classical motif used in a most unclassical way. The set was presented to Nicholas Dean, president of the Croton Aqueduct Department, in 1852.

Another pitcher with political associations *(Fig. 256)*, two years later than the Bard and Lamont abolitionist example already illustrated *(see Fig. 243)*, has even more extravagant overlaid decoration. The chased scene of a Whig meeting is swamped by bold ornament that extends over neck and foot. Made by Osmon Reed, (worked *ca.* 1840–50) of Philadelphia, it was presented to the governor of Tennessee in 1843. Classical urns also appeared about this time; one of these was made by William Forbes for Ball, Tompkins and Black of New York *(Fig. 257)*. Set on freely decorated and pierced Rococo feet, the urn has pierced, florid sides, and a heavily ornamented cover. It is dated 1841, the same year as the Philadelphia pitcher by Bard and Lamont *(see Fig. 243)*; in the latter example, the form better survives the incursions of the proliferating decoration.

Three tea sets of a basically similar form

253

253. Punch bowl, *ca.* 1895–1905, by the Gorham Company; L. 17⅝ inches. (Whereabouts unknown.) Photograph courtesy of the Gorham Company, Providence, Rhode Island.

254

255

254. Gold vase, 1893–95, by Paulding Farnham for Tiffany and Company; H. 19½ inches. The Metropolitan Museum of Art, New York. Gift of Edward D. Adams, 1904.

255. Pitcher and goblets, *ca.* 1840–50, by William Adams; H. (pitcher) 16 inches. Formerly collection of Joseph B. Brenauer. Photograph courtesy of Museum of the City of New York.

256. Pitcher, 1843, by Osmon Reed; H. 17¾ inches. Philadelphia Museum of Art. Purchased: Temple Fund (Acc. no. 02-6).

257. Urn, 1841, by William Forbes for Ball, Tompkins and Black; H. 10¾ inches. Owned by The Henry Ford Museum, Dearborn, Michigan.

257

256

258

illustrated here show some of the varieties
of decoration available in the 1840's and
1850's. Each has the inverted-pear shape
of the later Rococo. One, washed with
gold *(Fig. 258)* and having restrained
borders of machine-rolled bands of naturalistic decoration, relies on lavish color
for its effect. The second *(Fig. 259)* is
smothered with scrolls, plants, and flowers,
with an unrelated classical decorative
band on the foot. The third *(Fig. 260)* has
gadrooning on cover and feet, a motif that
becomes rather ponderous at the lip of
each vessel.

Further expressions of the Rococo revival are found in two pieces, one of
which *(Fig. 261)* is virtually a reproduction of a fully developed Rococo object
(see Fig. 149). Details of the ornament on
the spout and the proportion of the size of
the decoration to the size of the object are
indications of the century's difference between these two pieces. The other object
(Fig. 262) is more typical of the Rococo

revival in form and decoration, but it is
set on ludicrously small feet, which throw
the whole object off balance.

It is a short step from the sagging pear
shape of this piece to the more sprightly
octagonal, pyriform tea set *(Fig. 263)* by
William F. Ladd (worked *ca.* 1830–45).
This set is nevertheless endowed with an
Eastern (Moorish) aspect by the long
neck of the pots and the sharp quality of
the engraving; the latter is still Rococo in
style, however, as are the scroll feet. A
pleasing variant of this type *(Fig. 264)*
was devised by R. and W. Wilson of
Philadelphia (worked *ca.* 1825–46); here·
the facets are curved and the base has
delicate applied Rococo ornament.

Boston silver of the later nineteenth
century was frequently restrained (a traditional characteristic, as we have seen,
and all to the good in this era). An ornate
yet still elegant cake basket *(Fig. 265)* is
a good illustration of these qualities. Compared to the floridly ornamented tea set

259

260

261

258. Gold-washed tea and coffee set, *ca.* 1840–50, by Edwin Stebbins and Company; H. (teapot) 11¾ inches. Owned by The Henry Ford Museum, Dearborn, Michigan.

259. Tea set, *ca.* 1830–40, by Marquand and Company for Ball, Tompkins and Black; H. (teapot) 10 inches. Courtesy of The New-York Historical Society, New York City.

260. Tea set, *ca.* 1840–50, by Gerardus Boyce; H. (teapot) 10⅝ inches. Courtesy of The New-York Historical Society, New York City.

261. Coffeepot, *ca.* 1848–58, by Lincoln and Foss; H. 11¼ inches. Collection of Mr. and Mrs. Denison Hatch, Riverside, Connecticut. Photograph courtesy of Gebelein Silversmiths, Boston.

262. Teapot, *ca.* 1850, by Jones, Ball and Company; H. *ca.* 9¾ inches. Worcester Art Museum, Worcester, Massachusetts. Bequest of Stephen Salisbury III.

263. Tea and coffee set, *ca.* 1835–45, by William F. Ladd; H. (coffeepot) 11 inches. Courtesy of The New-York Historical Society, New York City.

264. Coffeepot and sugar bowl, *ca.* 1830–45, by R. and W. Wilson; H. (coffeepot) 10½ inches. (Whereabouts unknown.) Photograph courtesy of Gebelein Silversmiths, Boston.

265. Cake basket, *ca.* 1835–45, by Jones, Ball and Poor; H. 4½ inches. Collection of Mr. and Mrs. John E. Ebert, Wellesley Hills, Massachusetts. Photograph courtesy of Gebelein Silversmiths, Boston.

266. Tea set, *ca.* 1835–45, by R. and W. Wilson; H. (teapot) 8⅘ inches. Philadelphia Museum of Art. Bequest of Joseph Bunford Samuel (Acc. no. 29-38-1,2,3,4).

262

263

264

265

266

267

267. Tea and coffee set, *ca.* 1850–60, by William Gale and Son; H. (coffeepot) 11¼ inches. Collection of Mr. and Mrs. Clinton P. Russell, Jr., Dallas, Texas. Photograph courtesy of Gebelein Silversmiths, Boston.

268. Teakettle on stand, *ca.* 1840–50, by Ball, Tompkins and Black; H. 13 inches. The Metropolitan Museum of Art, New York. Gift of Mr. and Mrs. Henry Mali, 1944.

269. Pitcher, 1857, by J. E. Caldwell and Company; H. 10⅛ inches. Philadelphia Museum of Art. Given by Mrs. Walter S. Detwiler (Acc. no. 65-136-1).

270. Tea set, *ca.* 1890–96, by Samuel Kirk and Son; H. (teapot) *ca.* 10 inches. (Whereabouts unknown.) Photograph courtesy of Gebelein Silversmiths, Boston.

269

270

271

272

273

238

274

271. Tazza, 1866, by the Gorham Company; H. 16¾ inches. Museum of the City of New York. Gift of Newcomb Carlton.

272. Covered dish, 1866, by the Gorham Company; H. 15⅛ inches. Museum of the City of New York. Gift of Newcomb Carlton.

273. Sauceboat, *ca.* 1850–60, by William Gale, Jr., and Company; H. 6¾ inches. Owned by The Henry Ford Museum, Dearborn, Michigan.

274. Tea and coffee set, *ca.* 1840–50, by Gale and Willis; H. (coffeepot) 11⅞ inches. Courtesy of The New-York Historical Society, New York City.

---

by R. and W. Wilson in the Philadelphia Museum *(Fig. 266)*, the virtues of the cake basket are fully apparent. A further comparison, this time with a New York set *(Fig. 267)* by William Gale and Son that attains a nadir of taste we have not observed before, is convincing proof.

Large objects like teakettles could withstand the welter of Rococo ornament characteristic of mid-nineteenth-century design. One such piece by Ball, Tompkins and Black *(Fig. 268)* is chaste by comparison with the William Gale tea set. The elaborate decoration enhances the curvilinear octagonal form *(see Fig. 264)*. A variant of this shape was chosen by J. E. Caldwell and Company of Philadel-

phia for a large pitcher presented to Captain Nobre of the barque *Irma*, in 1857 *(Fig. 269)*. Instead of Rococo foliage, however, the pitcher is decorated with large water lilies in relief, which prefigure the designs of William Morris and Art Nouveau.

A monument of repulsiveness in nineteenth-century silver, and an excellent illustration of the misunderstanding of earlier styles, is a tea set *(Fig. 270)* made by Samuel Kirk and Son between 1890 and 1896. The classical forms are overlaid to an unprecedented extent with elaborate Rococo *repoussé* ornament.

Many of the elements invoked in the revival of the Renaissance bear as distant a relationship to the original as those in the earlier Rococo revival. Classical motifs were still freely used: A tazza (or salver) and dish presented to Cyrus Field by George Peabody in 1866, for his efforts in the completion of an Atlantic cable, may be cited as illustrations of this *(Figs. 271 and 272)*. Applied cherub handles interfere with the clear profile of the shallow bowl of the tazza, and the base and the stem are fashioned in the form of a figure of Columbia on a globe, surmounting a beaded cone with medallions, leafy

275

275. Pitcher and sugar bowl, 1870, by Crosby and Foss; H. (pitcher) *ca.* 7 inches. Photograph courtesy of Gebelein Silversmiths, Boston.

276. Coffeepot, *ca.* 1863–67, by Shreve and Vanderslice; H. 12⅛ inches. California Historical Society, San Francisco.

277. Candlesticks and pitcher, *ca.* 1890–1900, by Goodnow and Jenks; H. (candlesticks) 9¼ inches. Collection of Gebelein Silversmiths, Boston.

278. Tea set, 1874, by Shreve and Company; H. (teapot) 10⅝ inches. California Historical Society, San Francisco.

277

278

border, and bracket feet. The covered dish is more restrained, although the wide band of decoration—oak leaves and stalks of wheat on a punched ground, with medallions similar to those on the tazza—may not be considered completely appropriate with the lion, the masks, and the Greek fret.

What might have been a beautifully poised classical sauceboat, with restrained Greek fret ornament on lip and foot, was spoiled by the addition to the handle of an irrelevant stag's head and a pineapple finial *(Fig. 273)*. The service made about 1840–50 by Gale and Willis of New York,

(Fig. 274), surely epitomizes the misreading of the classical aesthetic. Purer forms were certainly made at this time, although they are tantamount to reproductions: Crosby and Foss of Boston could make a fine classical pitcher and sugar bowl in 1870 *(Fig. 275)*; in California in the 1860's, Shreve and Vanderslice could create a classical coffeepot with the ubiquitous Greek fret *(Fig. 276)*; and, at the very end of the century, classical candlesticks and a half-breed Empire pitcher were among forms made by Goodnow and Jenks of Boston *(Fig. 277)*.

Some of the aesthetic tenets of East-

279

280

279. Cream jug and sugar bowl, 1874, by Tiffany and Company; H. (sugar bowl) 5 inches. The Metropolitan Museum of Art, New York. Edgar J. Kaufmann Charitable Foundation Fund, 1969.

280. Candelabrum, 1890, Tiffany and Company; H. 21½ inches. Museum of the City of New York. Gift in memory of Daisy Beard Brown by her daughters, Bertha Shults Dougherty and Isabel Shults.

281. Letter-opener, brooch, belt buckle, *ca.* 1895–1905, by Unger Brothers; L. (letter-opener) 9⅞ inches. The Metropolitan Museum of Art, New York. Gift of Ronald S. Kane, 1967.

282. Hand mirror, *ca.* 1895–1905, by Tiffany and Company; L. 10¼ inches. Collection of The Museum of Modern Art, New York. Gift of Joseph H. Heil.

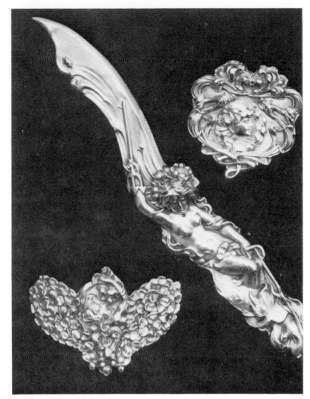

281

282

lake mingled with an Oriental decorativeness can be found in two services of the mid-1870's. The more complete set *(Fig. 278)* was made by Shreve and Company of San Francisco in 1874. Spare forms and clear profiles were enhanced with admirably restrained decoration. The engraved foliage ornaments the surface to the same extent as the more obviously Oriental applied decorations on the Tiffany set *(Fig. 279)*.

Among Oriental motifs popular in the last quarter of the century was the chrysanthemum, symbol of longevity. It ornaments a superb candelabrum—of definite eighteenth-century derivation—on the base, stem, and branches *(Fig. 280)*. The naturalistic decoration bears an excellent relation to the form, so that both are

283

284

285

286

283. Vase, *ca.* 1890–1910, by Alvin Manufacturing Company; H. 12¼ inches. The Metropolitan Museum of Art, New York. Anonymous Gift Fund, 1968.

284. Punch set, *ca.* 1900, by the Gorham Company; D. (plateau) 26½ inches. (Whereabouts unknown.) Photograph courtesy of the Gorham Company, Providence, Rhode Island.

285. Tea and coffee set, *ca.* 1900, by the Gorham Company; H. (coffeepot) 9½ inches. (Whereabouts unknown.) Photograph courtesy of the Gorham Company, Providence, Rhode Island.

286. Gold cup, 1900, by Karl Bitter (made by William B. Durgin Company); H. 14⁷⁄₁₆ inches. The Metropolitan Museum of Art, New York. Gift of Marcus I. Goldman, 1948.

clearly comprehensible. This object—the pattern was introduced in 1880—was part of a wedding-present set of more than one hundred and fifty pieces made by Tiffany and Company in 1890.

Small, intimate, Art Nouveau objects exemplify the pleasurable or sensuous qualities that the style was meant to impart *(Fig. 281)*. Delicate, languid naturalism can be seen in the letter-opener and brooch, while the intensified sensuality of the style is well illustrated by the butterfly-shaped belt buckle, ornamented with a female head with long flowing hair surrounded by (presumably) thickly fragrant flowers. All three objects were made by Unger Brothers of Newark, New Jersey (1881–1910), who specialized in Art Nouveau trinkets. The familiar Art Nouveau peacock makes its appearance on a small Tiffany hand mirror of silver, enamel, and sapphires *(Fig. 282)*. The long, flowing handle and the borders of the mirror are typical of the style, the linear delicacy and spareness of which may also be seen in a glass vase *(Fig. 283)* with a design in the silver-deposit process (created by electroplating a design that had been previously applied to the glass with silver flux). The shape of the slender, almost classical vase is an excellent foil for the spare, slender elegance of the silver design. How much more restrained and effective is this than such Art Nouveau designs as the over-elaborate Martelé punch bowl by the Gorham Company *(Fig. 284)*. Here the clarity of line is unfortunately obscured by a profusion of detail. Another Martelé set *(Fig. 285)* reveals an unsure hand at work with familiar Art Nouveau motifs—the sweeping precision that is necessary for the best results in this style is lacking.

Typifying the Beaux-Arts tradition is the work in gold of one of the chief designers of that movement, Karl Bitter, who was a friend and colleague of its leading architect, Richard Morris Hunt. Designed by Bitter, the cup *(Fig. 286)* was made by the William Durgin Company of Concord, New Hampshire, for the golden wedding anniversary in 1900 of Marcus and Bertha Goldman. On a base replete with classical motifs is seated Eros, who supports two entwined tree trunks bearing leafy branches. The union and procreativeness is further expressed in relief roundels on the solidly classical bowl of the cup—marriage, children, grandchildren, with winged classical figures between the roundels.

American silver is still being made. Fine pieces in a modern style have been fashioned in many cities in America in the last few generations, and individual silversmiths as well as large commercial operations are still active. But so much work remains to be done into all late-nineteenth- and early-twentieth-century decorative arts that it is not yet possible to produce a fully adequate survey of those times. Moreover, it is only too obvious that silver has lost its old social significance, as it lost its former economic importance in the nineteenth century. The new synthetic materials, with their durability and easier maintenance, have largely replaced silver in the home, while the greater availability of modern fine arts in all media has tended to swamp most inclination for contemporary silver objects as art forms. Yet the collecting of old silver is more widespread than ever. There is, after all, a profound pleasure and a spiritual enlightenment to be gained from the sense of the individual qualities of old silver; the perception of a very personal involvement in the original designing, making, and owning of it. As you hold it and turn it over in your hands you might almost feel you are approaching the man who made it. And as you contemplate it you may come to comprehend the lovely synthesis of scale and proportion, form and ornament that the best of it achieves.

Bibliography

GENERAL

AVERY, C. LOUISE. *American Silver of the XVII and XVIII Centuries: A Study Based on the Clearwater Collection.* Preface by R. T. HAINES HALSEY. New York: The Metropolitan Museum of Art, 1920.

————. *Early American Silver.* Reprint. New York: Russell and Russell, 1969. (First published in 1930; New York: The Century Company.)

BIGELOW, FRANCIS HILL. *Historic Silver of the Colonies and Its Makers.* New edition. New York: Tudor Publishing Company, 1948. (First published in 1917; New York: The Macmillan Company.)

BOHAN, PETER, and HAMMERSLOUGH, PHILIP. *Early Connecticut Silver, 1700–1840.* Middletown, Conn.: Wesleyan University Press, 1970.

BUCK, JOHN HENRY. *Old Plate, Its Makers & Marks.* Second edition. New York: The Gorham Manufacturing Company, 1903.

BUHLER, KATHRYN C. *American Silver.* Cleveland and New York: The World Publishing Company, 1950.

————. *Massachusetts Silver in the Frank L. and Louise C. Harrington Collection.* Worcester, Mass.: Barre Publishers, 1965.

————. *Mount Vernon Silver.* Mount Vernon, Va.: Mount Vernon Ladies' Association of the Union, 1957.

————. *Paul Revere, Goldsmith.* Boston: Museum of Fine Arts, 1956.

————, and HOOD, GRAHAM. *American Silver, Garvan and Other Collections, in the Yale University Art Gallery.* New Haven, Conn.: Yale University Art Gallery, 1970.

CLARKE, HERMANN FREDERICK. *John Coney, Silversmith 1655–1722.* With Introduction by HOLLIS FRENCH. Boston: Houghton Mifflin Company, 1932.

————. *John Hull, A Builder of the Bay Colony.* Portland, Me.: The Southworth-Anthoensen Press, 1940.

————, and FOOTE, HENRY WILDER. *Jeremiah Dummer, Colonial Craftsman and Merchant 1645–1718.* With Foreword by E. ALFRED JONES. Boston: Houghton Mifflin Company, 1935.

CURRIER, ERNEST M. *Marks of Early American Silversmiths.* Edited by KATHRYN C. BUHLER. Portland, Me.: The Southworth-Anthoensen Press, 1938.

ENSKO, STEPHEN G. C. *American Silversmiths and Their Marks.* 3 volumes. New York: Privately printed, 1927, 1937, 1948.

FALES, MARTHA GANDY. *American Silver in the Henry Francis du Pont Winterthur*

Museum. Winterthur, Del.: The Henry Francis du Pont Winterthur Museum, 1958.

————. *Early American Silver for the Cautious Collector.* New York: Funk and Wagnalls, 1970.

FLYNT, HENRY N., and FALES, MARTHA GANDY. *The Heritage Foundation Collection of Silver: With Biographical Sketches of New England Silversmiths, 1625–1825.* Old Deerfield, Mass.: The Heritage Foundation, 1968.

FORBES, ESTHER. *Paul Revere and the World He Lived In.* Boston: Houghton Mifflin Company, 1942.

FRENCH, HOLLIS. *Jacob Hurd and His Sons Nathaniel and Benjamin, Silversmiths, 1702–1781.* With a Foreword by KATHRYN C. BUHLER. Printed for The Walpole Society. Cambridge, Mass.: Riverside Press, 1939.

HAMMERSLOUGH, PHILIP H. *American Silver, Collected by Philip H. Hammerslough.* 3 volumes, with two supplements. Hartford, Conn.: Privately printed, 1958, 1960, 1965.

HIPKISS, EDWIN J. *Eighteenth-Century American Arts. The M. and M. Karolik Collection.* Published for the Museum of Fine Arts, Boston. Cambridge, Mass.: Harvard University Press, 1941.

————. *The Philip Leffingwell Spalding Collection of Early American Silver.* Published for the Museum of Fine Arts, Boston. Cambridge, Mass.: Harvard University Press, 1943.

JACKSON, CHARLES JAMES. *History of English Plate.* London: Country Life Ltd. and B. T. Batsford, 1911.

JONES, E. ALFRED. *The Old Silver of American Churches.* Letchworth, England: National Society of Colonial Dames of America, 1913.

————. *Old Silver of Europe and America.* Philadelphia: J. B. Lippincott Company, 1928.

KAUFFMANN, HENRY J. *The Colonial Silversmith: His Techniques and His Products.* Camden, N.J.: Thomas Nelson, Inc., 1969.

Kirk Silver in U.S. Museums. Baltimore, Md.: Samuel Kirk and Son, 1967.

KOVEL, RALPH M. and TERRY H. *American Silver, Pewter and Silver Plate.* New York: Crown Publishers, 1961.

McCLINTON, KATHARINE MORRISON. *Collecting American Nineteenth-Century Silver.* New York: Charles Scribner's Sons, 1968.

MATTEO, WILLIAM DE. *The Silversmith in Eighteenth-Century Williamsburg.* Williamsburg, Va.: Colonial Williamsburg, Inc., 1956.

OKIE, HOWARD PITCHER. *Old Silver and Old Sheffield Plate.* First edition. Garden City, N.Y.: Doubleday, Doran and Company, Inc., 1928.

OMAN, CHARLES. *English Domestic Silver.* London: Adam and Charles Black, 1962.

PETERSON, HAROLD L. *The American Sword 1775–1945.* Philadelphia: Privately printed, 1955.

PHILLIPS, JOHN MARSHALL. *American Silver.* New York: Chanticleer Press, 1949.

————. *Early American Silver Selected from the Mabel Brady Garvan Collection.* Edited with Introduction and notes by MEYRIC R. ROGERS, New Haven, Conn.: Yale University Art Gallery, 1960.

————. *The Hundred Masterpieces of American Silver in Public Collections.* Offprint. First published in *Antiques,* LIV (December, 1948), 412–16; LV (February, April, 1949), 116–20, 281–85; LVI (July, 1949), 41–45.

RAINWATER, DOROTHY T. *American Silver Manufacturers.* Hanover, Pa.: Everybody's Press, 1966.

ROSENBAUM, JEANNETTE. *Myer Myers, Goldsmith, 1723–1795.* Philadelphia: Jewish Publication Society of America, 1954.

SINGLETON, ESTHER. *Dutch New York.* New York: Dodd, Mead and Company, 1909.

THORN, C. JORDAN. *Handbook of American Silver and Pewter Marks.* Preface by JOHN M. GRAHAM, II. New York: Tudor Publishing Company, 1949.

WENHAM, EDWARD. *The Practical Book of American Silver.* First Edition. Philadelphia: J. B. Lippincott, 1949.

WYLER, SEYMOUR B. *The Book of Old Silver.* New York: Crown Publishers, 1937.

REGIONAL STUDIES

CONNECTICUT

CURTIS, GEORGE MUNSON. *Early Silver of Connecticut and Its Makers.* Meriden, Conn.: International Silver Company, 1913.

DELAWARE

HARRINGTON, JESSIE. *Silversmiths of Delaware, 1700–1850.* Camden, N.J.: National Society of Colonial Dames of America in the State of Delaware, 1939.

GEORGIA

CUTTEN, GEORGE BARTON. *Silversmiths of Georgia, 1733–1850.* Savannah, Ga.: The Pigeonhole Press, 1958.

KENTUCKY

HIATT, NOBLE W., and LUCY F. *The Silversmiths of Kentucky, 1785–1850.* Introduction by J. WINSTON COLEMAN, JR. First edition. Louisville, Ky.: Standard Print Company, 1954.

MARYLAND

PLEASANTS, J. HALL, and SILL, HOWARD. *Maryland Silversmiths 1715–1830.* Baltimore, 1930.

NEW JERSEY

WILLIAMS, CARL M. *Silversmiths of New Jersey, 1700–1825. With Some Notice of Clockmakers Who Were Also Silversmiths.* Philadelphia: George S. MacManus Company, 1949.

NEW YORK

Darling Foundation (Herbert F. Darling, President). *New York State Silversmiths.* IRVING D. WOODIN, initiator and adviser. New York, 1964.

NORTH CAROLINA

CUTTEN, GEORGE BARTON. *Silversmiths of North Carolina.* Raleigh, N.C.: State Department of Archives and History, 1948.

OHIO

KNITTLE, RHEA MANSFIELD. *Early Ohio Silversmiths and Pewterers, 1787–1847.* Cleveland, Ohio: Calvert-Hatch Company, 1943.

PENNSYLVANIA *(Philadelphia)*

BRIX, MAURICE. *List of Philadelphia Silversmiths and Allied Artificers, from 1682 to 1850.* Philadelphia: Privately printed, 1920.

RHODE ISLAND

CARPENTER, RALPH E., JR. *Arts and Crafts of Newport, R.I., 1640–1820.* Newport, R.I.: The Preservation Society of Newport County, 1954.

SOUTH CAROLINA

BURTON, E. MILBY. *South Carolina Silversmiths 1690–1860.* Charleston, S.C.: The Charleston Museum, 1942.

VIRGINIA

CUTTEN, GEORGE BARTON. *Silversmiths of Virginia, 1694–1850.* Richmond, Va.: Dietz Press, 1952.

MAJOR EXHIBITIONS OF AMERICAN SILVER AND THEIR CATALOGUES

American Silver, The Work of Seventeenth- and Eighteenth-Century Silversmiths. Museum of Fine Arts, Boston. Introduction by R. T. Haines Halsey. 1906.

Hudson-Fulton Exhibition. The Metropolitan Museum of Art, New York. Henry Watson Kent and Florence N. Levy. 1909.

American Church Silver. Museum of Fine Arts, Boston. Introduction by George M. Curtis. 1911.

Silver Used in New York, New Jersey and the South. The Metropolitan Museum of Art, New York. Introduction by R. T. Haines Halsey. 1911.

Loan Exhibition of Silver. Pennsylvania Museum of Art. Samuel W. Woodhouse, Jr. 1921.

Philadelphia Silver. Rooms of the National Society of Colonial Dames, Philadelphia. 1929. Objects included in Mrs. Alfred

Coxe Prime, *Three Centuries of Historic Silver* (Philadelphia, 1938).

Early New York Silver. The Metropolitan Museum of Art, New York. C. Louise Avery. 1931–32.

Early Connecticut Silver. Gallery of Fine Arts, Yale University. John Marshall Phillips. 1935.

Harvard Tercentenary Exhibition. Harvard University. 1936.

Silver by New York Makers, Late Seventeenth Century to 1900. Museum of the City of New York. V. Isabelle Miller. 1937–38.

Masterpieces of New England Silver. Gallery of Fine Arts, Yale University. John Marshall Phillips. 1939.

Exhibition of Silver—French, British, American, Modern. Virginia Museum of Fine Arts, Richmond. Edward Morris Davis, III. 1940.

Early American Silver. Wadsworth Atheneum, Hartford, Conn. Philip H. Hammerslough. 1945.

American Silverware of the Seventeenth and Eighteenth Centuries. Part of "From Colony to Nation" exhibition, Art Institute of Chicago. Meyric R. Rogers. 1949.

Silver by Early Connecticut Makers. Wadsworth Atheneum, Hartford, Conn. Philip H. Hammerslough. 1954.

American Silver Mounted Swords. Corcoran Gallery of Art, Washington, D.C. Harold L. Peterson. 1954.

Colonial Silversmiths, Masters, and Apprentices. Museum of Fine Arts, Boston. Kathryn C. Buhler. 1956.

French, English, and American Silver, A Loan Exhibition in Honor of Russell A. Plimpton. Minneapolis Institute of Arts. Kathryn C. Buhler. 1956.

Philadelphia Silver 1682–1800. Philadelphia Museum of Art. Henry P. McIlhenny, Introduction by Mrs. A. C. Prime. 1956.

New Hampshire Silver, 1775–1825. Currier Gallery of Art, Manchester, N.H. Charles E. Buckley. 1957.

Elias Pelletreau. The Brooklyn Museum. Marvin C. Schwartz. 1959.

An Exhibition of American Silver and Art Treasures. English-Speaking Union, at Christie's Great Rooms, London. Kathryn C. Buhler. 1960.

Masterpieces of American Silver. Virginia Museum of Fine Arts, Richmond. Kathryn C. Buhler. 1960.

Early Silver in California Collections. Los Angeles County Museum of Art. Gregor Norman-Wilcox. 1962.

New York Silversmiths of the Seventeenth Century. Museum of the City of New York. V. Isabelle Miller. 1962–63.

American Art from American Collections. The Metropolitan Museum of Art. James Biddle. 1963.

American Gold 1700–1860. Yale University Art Gallery. Peter J. Bohan. 1963.

Classical America. Newark Museum. William H. Gerdts and Berry B. Tracy. 1963.

Albany Silver 1652–1825. Albany Institute of History and Art. Norman S. Rice. 1964.

Myer Myers: American Silversmith. The Jewish Museum, New York City. Thomas L. Freudenheim. 1965.

The New England Silversmith. Museum of Art, Rhode Island School of Design, Providence. Hugh J. Gourley, III. 1965.

A Century of Alexandria, District of Columbia and Georgetown Silver, 1750–1850. Corcoran Gallery of Art, Washington, D.C. 1966.

Samuel Kirk and Son: American Silver Craftsmen Since 1815. Chicago Historical Society. 1966.

Silver in Newark. Newark Museum. J. Stewart Johnson. 1966.

An Exhibition of Early Silver Made by New Haven Silversmiths. New Haven Colony Historical Society, New Haven, Conn. John D. Kernan. 1967.

Southern Silver, An Exhibition of Silver Made in the South Prior to 1860. The Museum of Fine Arts, Houston, Tex. David B. Warren. 1968.

Nineteenth Century America: Furniture and Other Decorative Arts. The Metropolitan Museum of Art, New York. Berry B. Tracy *et al.* 1970.

Significant Public Collections of American Silver

Albany Institute of History and Art, Albany, N.Y.

Bayou Bend Collection, Museum of Fine Arts, Houston, Tex.

The Brooklyn Museum, N.Y.

The Cleveland Museum of Art, Ohio

Colonial Williamsburg, Va.

Currier Gallery of Art, Manchester, N.H.

The Detroit Institute of Arts, Mich.

William Hayes Fogg Art Museum, Harvard University, Cambridge, Mass.

Henry Ford Museum, Dearborn, Mich.

The Henry Francis du Pont Winterthur Museum, Winterthur, Del.

The Heritage Foundation, Old Deerfield, Mass.

The Metropolitan Museum of Art, New York, N.Y.

The Minneapolis Institute of Arts, Minn.

Museum of the City of New York, N.Y.

Museum of Fine Arts, Boston, Mass.

The New-York Historical Society, N.Y.

Philadelphia Museum of Art, Pa.

Rhode Island School of Design, Museum of Art, Providence, R.I.

Smithsonian Institution, Washington, D.C.

Sterling and Francine Clark Art Institute, Williamstown, Mass.

Virginia Museum of Fine Arts, Richmond, Va.

Wadsworth Atheneum, Hartford, Conn.

Worcester Art Museum, Mass.

Yale University Art Gallery, New Haven, Conn.

Index